WORKING RECLAIMED WOOD

WORKING RECLAIMED WOOD

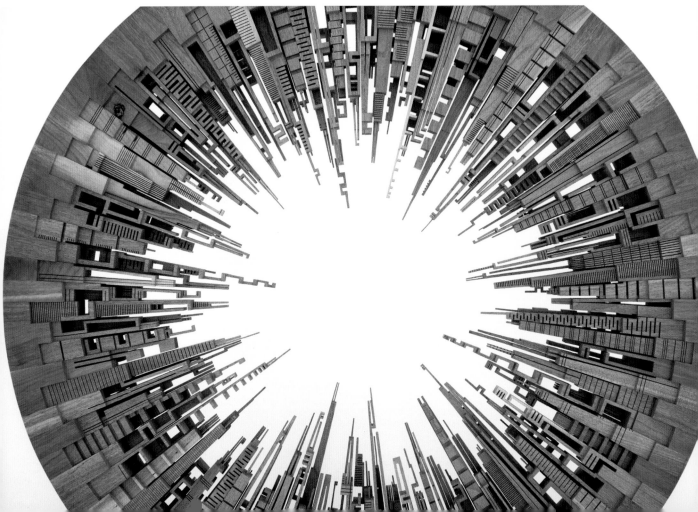

Working Reclaimed Wood

A Guide for Woodworkers, Makers & Designers

Yoav Liberman

POPULAR WOODWORKING BOOKS
CINCINNATI, OHIO
www.popularwoodworking.com

Distributed in the U.K. and Europe by
F&W Media International
Pynes Hill Court
Pynes Hill
Rydon Lane
Exeter
EX2 5AZ
United Kingdom
Tel: (+44) 1392 797680

Visit our website at popularwoodworking.com or our consumer website at shopwoodworking.com for more woodworking information.

Other fine Popular Woodworking Books are available from your local bookstore or direct from the publisher.

ISBN-13: 978-1-4403-5081-8

22 21 20 19 18   5 4 3 2 1

EDITOR: A.J. Hamler
INTERIOR DESIGNER: Wendy Dunning
PRODUCTION COORDINATOR: Debbie Thomas
COVER PHOTOS: Multi-color table photo by Moshi Gitelis.
All other photos by the author.
"Torah Ark" by Yoav Liberman (2014)
Reclaimed woods, reclaimed glass window,
reclaimed brass hardware, 67" x 20" x 14"

a content + ecommerce company

Read this important safety notice

To prevent accidents, keep safety in mind while you work. Use the safety guards installed on power equipment; they are for your protection. When working on power equipment, keep fingers away from saw blades, wear safety goggles to prevent injuries from flying wood chips and sawdust, wear ear protectors, and consider installing a dust vacuum to reduce the amount of airborne sawdust in your woodshop. Don't wear loose clothing, such as neckties or shirts with loose sleeves, or jewelry, such as rings, necklaces or bracelets, when working on power equipment. Tie back long hair to prevent it from getting caught in your equipment. People who are sensitive to certain chemicals should check the chemical content of any product before using it. The author and editors who compiled this book have tried to make the contents as accurate and correct as possible. Plans, illustrations, photographs and text have been carefully checked. All instructions, plans and projects should be carefully read, studied and understood before beginning construction. Due to the variability of local conditions, construction materials, skill levels, etc., neither the author nor Popular Woodworking Books assumes any responsibility for any accidents, injuries, damages or other losses incurred resulting from the material presented in this book. Prices listed for supplies and equipment were current at the time of publication and are subject to change. Glass shelving should have all edges polished and must be tempered. Untempered glass shelves may shatter and can cause serious bodily injury. Tempered shelves are very strong and if they break will just crumble, minimizing personal injury.

METRIC CONVERSION CHART

to convert	to	multiply by
Inches	Centimeters	2.54
Centimeters	Inches	0.4
Feet	Centimeters	30.5
Centimeters	Feet	0.03
Yards	Meters	0.9
Meters	Yards	1.1

Table of Contents

About This Book
Reclaimed Wood in the Age of Disposability

Self-preservation is one of the strongest forces in nature. While this is true of organisms that strive to overcome the difficulties that life presents to them, self-preservation – and its altruistic relative, preservation – is the force that motivates and leads me and my fellow reclaimers in our quest to allow nature's prime material, wood, to survive beyond its primal use and flourish again in new creations. We love to see rejected, tossed-away, abandoned or forgotten wood and timber acquire new life and become useful again in creations such as furniture, interiors and even building construction. The purpose of this book is to demonstrate the potential of reclaimed wood and other reclaimed materials. We'll examine how to "recruit" and rehabilitate them, then how to design and build with them.

"ETROG BOX" BY YOAV LIBERMAN (2005)
Longleaf pine, wenge, cherry, walnut, brass, silk and linen
padding, 9" x 5.5" x 8"
PHOTOGRAPH BY YOAV LIBERMAN

"CORDUROY" BY YOAV LIBERMAN (2001)
Douglas fir, polyurethane, 18.5" x 13.5" x 10"
PHOTOGRAPH BY GAIL HANDELMANN

"MULBERRY TRIO TABLE" BY YOAV LIBERMAN (2012)
Mulberry, oak, maple, mahogany, teak, steel, milk paint
36" x 17.5" x 52"
PHOTOGRAPH BY YOAV LIBERMAN

Reclaimed, reused, repurposed

I've been utilizing reclaimed material from the first day I became a woodworker. Reclaimed wood and found objects provide not only ecologically savvy raw material, but also the conceptual inspiration for the creation of new pieces. When I work with reclaimed materials I tap into the memories and experiences resonating from the reclaims. I look past flaws to mine the materials' rich aesthetic, functional and structural potential, challenging myself to bring these strengths to the fore. Working with reclaimed resources is an invigorating challenge that rewards the designer, the maker and the user with a piece that is imbued with history, environmental significance and one-of-a-kind charm.

This book explores furniture, decorative art and sculpture made from reclaimed materials – mostly wood. I'll show you how to resource materials, treat them, design according to what you obtain and, lastly, build your pieces. Whether you're a designer, maker, collector or simply an owner of furniture, you'll find the tools to understand, appreciate and build meaningful pieces that stem from the salvageable.

The definition of what is "reclaimed" wood can be quite broad. It can include wood that has been put to use at some point for one purpose – a structural beam from a Colonial era barn for instance. With the barn dismantled and the beams resawn, the planks can now be reconfigured and used to build new furniture. Other types of reclaimed projects can evolve from miscellaneous cutoffs, scraps and rejected virgin lumber,

to become something new. Reclaiming can also mean repurposing drift- and abandoned wood, logs and limbs salvaged from riverbanks and the woods.

To this family of "R" (reclaimed, recovered, reconfigured and repurposed materials) we can also add one more: reused. By this I mean incorporating complete parts such as a leg of a table or a rusted drawer handle rescued from the garbage to serve in new furniture. Those adopted objects can be subjected to some kind of cosmetic or structural modification before being incorporated into the new piece, or simply added as-is to showcase their unapologetic previously owned history at the fore.

For many makers, environmental considerations lead the

way toward choosing to incorporate reclaimed wood and materials in their projects. As we become more and more aware of the paramount importance of our environmental responsibilities as de facto guardians of this world, so arises the recognition that irresponsible harvesting, processing, utilizing and disposing of nature's precious resources all come with a price.

In other words, reclaimed wood is environmentally correct. Wood, as we know it, is one of the largest repositories for CO_2 – the prime suspect related to global warming. By reusing reclaimed wood we accomplish two important things: First, we reduce the wastefulness of dumping a great resource into our landfills, which will eventually decompose

and release CO2 back to the atmosphere. Reclaiming wood also helps moderate the purchase of new lumber, which, in turn, (hopefully) prevents further deforestation, allowing more trees to grow and flourish and absorb more CO2 from the atmosphere.

Special, by nature

After laying out the environmental rationale for why we should give preference to wood as a building material comes the question: What is so special in reclaimed wood beyond the morality of conservation and preservation?

In two words: Attributed (or associated) history. This last point is very subjective, but also very powerful. In many cases

reclaimed lumber will bare layers of patinated evidence that denotes use (or abuse). These wooden elements fossilize in them not only the physical growth history of an ancient tree, but also radiate the chronicles of decades or even centuries in which the lumber was put to use in buildings or in the furniture of origin.

To many it is the narrative of origin and growth, and the spirits of past companionship with humanity that gives the reclaim its meaning, which then bestow the new piece – built from it – with an added value of legacy, pedigree and beauty.

"TREES ARE POEMS THAT THE EARTH WRITES UPON THE SKY." – KAHLIL GIBRAN

Trees are absolutely majestic and deserve our utmost respect as facilitators of life. They bestow us with a bounty of gifts: shade, fruits, beauty and oxygen. They serve as a habitat and a source of nutrients for so many living beings. Then, when their time comes they can become our homes, furniture and many other objects of use and beauty.

While metals, follicle-driven materials and other quarried goods are finite, this is not the case with wood. Wood, together with other plant-based materials such as bamboo and fibers, can grow out of thin air. Well not exactly out of thin air, but really close to it. Give a seed some sunlight, water and carbon dioxide, then wait a few decades and nature's nursery will produce for us one of the strongest, most millable, richest and most diverse materials ever seen. Lumber is this fantastic stuff and woodworkers are its shapers.

This most noble of material treasures – wood, which not only freely "grows on trees," and transforms pollution into gold – is a dependable renewable resource that, if harvested and used with care, can provide for us happily ever after. Think about it, trees are so good at absorbing carbon

dioxide from the air and able via the magic of photosynthesis to convert it into oxygen and carbon. The oxygen that trees release allows us and all other living beings to breathe, while the carbon that the trees lock in their cells, together with a few other substances, become this wonderful building material – wood.

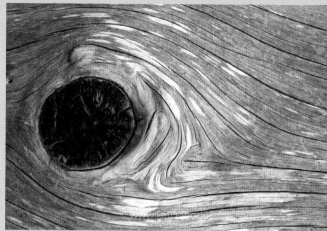

PHOTOGRAPHS BY DAN LIEBERMAN

THE MERRITT TABLE

In 2006, a heavy steel lab table was dismantled and tossed away from one of Harvard University's labs. Four years later the table's legs plus reclaimed heart pine from a salvaged beam came together to form the Merritt Table.

After wood, the materials I enjoy working with the most are steel, brass and bronze. Sometimes I "cast" steel components as "actors in a supporting role" in my furniture. In fact, steel and brass fasteners are instrumental in accentuating many of the construction and joining methods I use.

"MERRITT TABLE" BY YOAV LIBERMAN (2010)
Steel, longleaf pine, brass, paint, varnish., 32" x 27" x 44"
PHOTOGRAPHS BY BILL HOO

Ever since childhood I have been taken by metal engineering. During my high school years I studied many of the technologies that allow us to tame metals and manipulate them to our needs. I learned to cast, forge, mill, fold, weld, drill, rivet and tap steel, aluminum, brass and bronze. Since then I routinely make use of this knowledge to augment many of my furniture projects. I appreciate metals for both their strength and appearance, and am a self-professed geek of steel joinery. I just love to collect and play around with knobs, nuts, bolts and their ilk, and I constantly make efforts to improve existing ready-made fasteners and connectors so I can harness them into my wooden projects.

When I first noticed the dismantled old Army-green steel

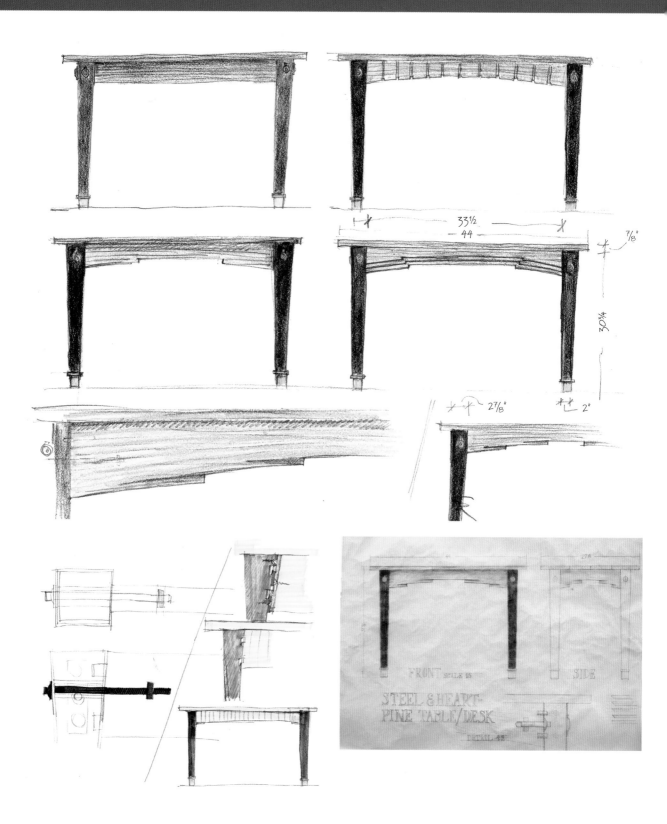

▲ Although discarded, the legs of the old table looked ready to enjoy a new life.

They don't look like much now, but once cleaned and cut some of the pieces of an old mill would make a perfect tabletop. ▶

desk outside its former lab I was ready to pick it up as a whole. But, I quickly realized that I didn't have the space nor the immediate use for it. Also, in my eyes at least, the only interesting parts of that desk were the legs. What appealed most to me was the heavy-gauge steel structure of the legs and the fact that they were capped with impressive feet of cast brass. So, I ended up saving the legs – I speculate the original designer was influenced by the Federal and Art Deco styles.

I shaped Merritt's wooden components from reclaimed longleaf pine beams which I saved from a pile of wood and brick debris that was all that was left of an old post-and-beam mill building leveled in Worcester, Mass., to make way for a road in the early 2000s. After salvaging the crippled beams and resawing them, they were ready for their next chapter in life as components of my new table.

The top of the new table is divided into two leaves connected with special panel bolts. I glued each leaf from a few

boards originating from the reclaimed beams.

It took me quite some time to design the Merritt aprons. I envisioned the apron beams as bridges spanning the legs, much like the many beautiful bridges that I saw on the Merritt Parkway in Connecticut on my visit to the USA back in 1997. I also wanted to make them look elegant using graduations. Graduation is a design principle common in Art Deco, a style that I respect very much. It is a very pronounced design element featured in works of art, architecture and design via steps or facets that dominate the object. Instead of a slope or a taper, many Art Deco objects are constructed and ornamented with lines or steps that change density, scale and size as they culminate into a terminal point or plane. I find this design expression quite attractive. It also goes remarkably well with the intrinsic grain, annual rings and lines found in wood – especially quartersawn lumber. To implement graduation in the Merritt aprons, I carved consecutive tapered steps

on the underside of the aprons.

After shaping the aprons I was ready to modify the legs as well as the robust catalog-bought bolts and nuts for the legs – my prefered fasteners for knockdown furniture – so they could reliably connect the legs to the aprons. After a few hours on a Bridgeport mill and a metal lathe, as well as some quiet time with files and sandpaper, the legs and fasteners were ready.

Next, I sent the steel legs to a professional auto body shop to be repainted while I finished the longleaf pine parts with oil-based varnish. Lastly, I installed new brass covers to cap the fastener holes in the legs which echo the polished brass feet of my reclaimed wood and found objects table.

2 | Before gluing up the tabletop leaf panels, cracks and other flaws are filled or glued

3 | The two leaves will be drilled to accept brass tabletop alignment pins.

4 | Laying out the aprons.

5 | Graduating the aprons.

6 | The author uses a metal lathe to reshape some ready-made knockdown fasteners.

7 | Although old, this Bridgeport mill easily helps produce table hardware.

CHAPTER 1

Reclaimed Wood

Definitions, subcategories, reasoning, types

Many people who show interest in reclaimed wood assume that reclaimed wood means "barn wood." But barn wood – timber, flooring and siding (or cladding) salvaged from dismantled barns or other farm structures – represents only one part of the reclaimed wood lexicon.

Sources for reclaimed wood span much wider than this, from sunken timber salvaged from the bottom of North America's lakes and rivers, to the dense Indonesian dunnage beams and battens acting as spacers between railroad rails shipped from Japan; from dismantled cedar staves that used to constitute old vinegar tanks, to mushroom-bed planks that show spectacular terrain and color.

Reclaimed wood originates from diverse sources and can come in a variety of shapes, physical and structural conditions, and historical pedigree. It can come in the form of small scraps, planks, sheets, slabs, boards, beams, columns and much, much more. This huge array of repurposed wood varies by species, physical and structural condition, and of course aesthetics. In order to help us learn about and distinguish between each subgroup of the reclaim menagerie, I created a classification system that divides the reclaimed wood into four groups: Heritage Reclaimed wood, Common Reclaimed wood, Salvaged/Recovered wood, and Recycled/Scrapped reclaims.

A ramshackle barn can have a second life when the building materials are repurposed into new creations.

An arsenal of equipment and personnel – including divers – raises timber submerged sometimes a century or more.
PHOTOGRAPH BY JOHN MORAN PHOTOGRAPHY

A typical haul when dismantling old mills might include these 12" x 14" beams.

PHOTOGRAPH BY MARC A. POIRIER

Old water towers, like this one in New York City, are a great source of reclaimed wood.

This bar stool was made entirely with wood repurposed from salvaged boats.

Massive old-growth trees were once a common sight in many parts of the word. Today, after centuries of over harvesting and forest decimation, hardly any old-growth trees remain (it becomes harder and harder to find these gentle giants in the developed world). Even more alarming, the combination of greed, ignorance and mismanagement has now placed the old-growth forests of the tropics, and many parts of Africa and Asia, on the verge of mass destruction. In this old photo, men stand with outstretched arms in front of the historic "Senator" cypress tree, demonstrating the massive girth of this enormous species of tree that used to grow to impressive size in Florida. This historic tree was later destroyed by fire in 2012.

The four types of reclaimed wood

Heritage Reclaimed wood

Heritage Reclaimed is the most prestigious and attractive of all reclaimed woods – rare, sometimes even finite in quantities, and exotic. It is lumber salvaged from historic barns, mill buildings, old wooden boats, water tanks, boardwalks and more. It is steeped in history, character, esteem and attributed value. Heritage reclaims carry the hallmarks of time and legacy, and often come from old-growth timber cut down many years ago. Heritage Reclaimed is coveted for its unique appearance that stems from the rarity of its core wood, or as a result of remarkable surface patina from years of use. Occasionally, Heritage Reclaimed will earn its rank thanks to unique circumstances such as in the case of a table built by Maria Pergay. The table's centerpiece is a slice of oak from a tree that was planted hundreds of years ago.

Iconic Paris-based designer Maria Pergay built this regal dining table around a very symbolic slice of wood from a tree planted in 1685 that became a favorite of Marie Antoinette, wife of Louis XVI of France. The tree survived not only the French Revolution and the Reign of Terror, but also both World Wars. It eventually succumbed to the forces of nature and fell in a catastrophic storm in 1999. Madam Pergay was able to procure some pieces of this historic tree and incorporated thin slices of the centuries-old oak into a few unique tables. This table features the last slice of oak available. It's a unique illustration of what I call the "Esteem" quality, attributed to some reclaimed woods.

Another example of Heritage Reclaimed wood is the old-growth claro walnut rifle blanks reconfigured by Wendy Maruyama to build the Bell Shrine cabinet in commemoration of elephants lost to poaching.

"TABLE MARIE ANTOINETTE," BY MARIA PERGAY (2016)
T-black stainless steel top, inlaid oak slice, mirrored stainless steel, lacquered black oak, glass, Plexiglas base.
32" x 138" x 64"
PHOTOGRAPHS BY THIERRY DEPAGNE. COURTESY OF DEMISCH DANANT

"BELL SHRINE" BY WENDY MARUYAMA (2015)
Claro walnut, holly, ink, bronze, 65" x 14" x 11"
PHOTOGRAPHS BY DAVID HARRISON

Wendy Maruyama's poetic cabinet "Bell Shrine" is a symbolic lamentation on the meaningless killing of elephants and rhinoceroses by poaching. Through this piece she tries to raise awareness and evoke empathy to the plight of the world's largest land animal. In an earnest irony, the beautiful old-growth claro walnut she used to build this piece came from reclaimed gunstock blanks, obtained from a rifle factory that had gone out of business. Her tall, somber cabinet protests the irrational hunger for ivory, which wreaks havoc on the African elephant to the point that on average a hundred elephants are killed every day solely for their tusks.

In her piece, modeled after a Buddhist shrine, a picture of an elephant is etched on the inner back. It is flanked on the right by a candle, representing unchanging truth (Dharma), and on the left by flowers, representing impermanence. An incense offering/burner is in the middle, as it relates to our spiritual state in the present moment. Above, a cast bronze bell, made by Sophie Glenn, rings every 15 minutes in honor of every elephant that loses its life to poaching. Maruyama, a celebrated studio-furniture maker, artist and scholar, voices a compassionate message that resonates clearly within and around this meaningful piece.

Sometimes, Heritage reclaims might serve the same purpose they served during their original use. For example, posts and beams salvaged from an old barn might be incorporated into the construction of a new building. Heart-pine floors from a vintage building might be recommissioned as floorboards in a new home or upscale restaurant.

As another example of this type of project, Gilad Erjaz incorporated reclaimed hewn post-and-beam components to enrich

▲ Reclaimer and designer Gilad Erjaz incorporated a variety of reclaimed lumber for this elegant restaurant.

◀ Designer Russell Piccione made use of reclaimed chestnut when building a new addition to a client's summerhouse in Shelter Island, N.Y. In this project, completed in 2013, reclaimed chestnut boards of exceptional width and provenance were used for the construction of both the floors and the wall paneling.

the design theme, and also to serve as structural weight-bearing elements, in a newly built Asian-style restaurant.

Of course, Heritage Reclaimed can also be repurposed to serve in different usages as well. After being cleaned and dried, for example, boards previously constituting mushroom beds might be installed as wall covers in a trendy coffee shop.

Heritage Reclaimed is often transformed for a totally new purpose. Cherished for their core wood, structural timber frame elements made from old-growth longleaf pine (heart pine) are often dismantled and reconfigured via sawing and milling to become dimensional boards from which new furniture and interior design elements are built. Teak pillars from Indonesian houses might be resawn into planks that give birth to a slick chest of drawers.

Common Reclaimed wood

Common Reclaimed wood is any used generic lumber materials derived from buildings, furniture or architectural woodwork that is being repurposed. Sources include lumber dismantled from newer buildings destined for demolition, cargo wood (hardwood, softwood and plywood from shipping pallets and crates), found furniture parts, bathroom and kitchen cabinets (doors, wooden countertops, etc.) left on the side of the road to be picked up by the trash truck.

Common Reclaimed may bare a coat of wood finish such as varnish or paint, but rarely displays patina, significant texture or aging. It is inexpensive or even free. In general, the lumber that yields this wood is not rare or extinct, unlike old-growth Heritage Reclaimed lumber.

Examples of this type of reclaimed wood usage: Strips of wood from a dismantled wooden pallet might be turned into parts for a futon bed. Pine roof rafters from a torn-down house can be glued together to make a workbench top. Doors discarded from a renovated kitchen might be incorporated into a newly built armoire.

◀ Lumber from an old pine bunk bed combines with curb-salvaged steel filing cabinets to create a petite but rock-solid workbench.

Designer Oded Keet's Pallet Wood and Steel-Base Table. Oded's table is a good personification of the potential and character of using Common Reclaimed wood – in this case from dismantled pallets. ▶

"SIX PACK LIGHT" BY YOAV LIBERMAN (2005)
Birch, wenge, brass, aluminum, 18" x 5.5" x 10"
PHOTOGRAPH BY DEAN POWELL

A log raft of heart pine floats down the Ocklawaha River in central Florida in July 1901, on it's way to a mill. Logs were sometimes lost and remained submerged for a century or more before recovery.

"PENLAND TABLE" BY YOAV LIBERMAN, PATRICK KANA (2012)
Soft Maple, poplar, 32" x 16" x 18"
PHOTOGRAPH BY YOAV LIBERMAN

Salvaged/Recovered wood

This is newly processed lumber that was saved from decomposition. A good example is "sinker" or sunken wood – logs that were inadvertently submerged more than a century ago in the waterways of North America on their way to the wood mill. Once brought to the surface they can be sawn and dried into magnificent planks. Driftwood is another example of this type of reclaimed wood. Trunks and branches that were swept into rivers and seas are naturally sculptured by the water over time and then drift ashore.

Salvaged wood can be obtained from fallen trees. Often these trees lie on the ground for some time before being claimed for a sculptural project or sawn into planks, and carry the evidences of marginalized decay and spalting as a result, which can make for interesting design features.

Recycled/Scrapped wood

These are repurposed scraps and cutoff pieces from woodworkers' shops, furniture manufacturers and lumber mills. Pieces of recycled wood can be amalgamated to create a new "canvas" of panels, beams and blocks, from which new pieces are created. Great recycled wood projects include cutting boards, segmented turned objects and small objects such as toys, handles and pens.

The author carved this walnut bowl (described in Chapter Five) from an oddly shaped block found in a shop scrap bin while teaching classes at Peters Valley School of Craft in Layton, N.J.

So, just what is it that makes reclaimed wood stand out when compared to new lumber? When looking to buy new wood for a project, most reputable woodworkers and enthusiastic amateurs aim for the best available grade of lumber. Our decision as to which type of wood to buy factor in the wood's intended use, strength, grain appearance and color. For an interior design or for a furniture project the greatest

The author's Mulberry Trio Table (profiled in Chapter Seven) features a top of salvaged wood quartersawn from a section of storm-felled mulberry tree, and these common reclaimed legs he found in a Dumpster.

A few of the author's handled cutting boards, made from recycled/scrapped maple and walnut firewood scraps and commercial lumber cutoffs. Smaller pieces of scrap can be turned on a lathe and then connected to bigger parts to make impressive, yet fully practical serving boards.

"CYPRESSTOOL" BY ODED KEET (2017)
Salvaged/recovered mediterranean cypress, 15" x 15" x 18"
PHOTOGRAPH BY ODED KEET

You can often find lumber cutoffs and odd-shaped 2nd-grade lumber that is problematic to sell at commercial lumber yards. Here at Condon Lumber in White Plains, N.Y., scrap bins are filled with discounted wood that can be put to great use.

emphasis is put upon the species appeal, cost and aesthetics. If your project's orientation gears mainly toward construction or it is an outdoor project, price, wood resiliency and strength govern your choices.

But when users, designers and makers consider reclaimed wood they do it mainly for four reasons: Ecology, Aesthetics, Esteem (the "story" or narrative of the wood) and Economy.

Tree debris on its way to the landfill.

Environment

Concern for our environment leads to conservation and preservation. This is one of the strongest motivations that attract people to reclaimed lumber, which is both rational and emotional. By buying reclaimed wood we believe that we help to preserve the lives of living trees and the forest's habitat, saving them and the lives that depend upon them from the reaper (or, in this case, the lumberjack). We also believe that we help in reducing the wastefulness of disposing and losing a perfectly viable resource that otherwise would have ended up buried in the landfill.

In addition, when we buy reclaimed wood we know we're helping to cultivate a market for it – which means that more people in the wood industry will view it as a commodity, and thus save, process and offer it for sale. We also know that if we display reclaimed wood and show its splendor, the people who are close to us and those we influence will learn to appreciate it too, and help further increase the demand for this wonderful resource. Reclaimed wood also resonates strongly with anyone who keeps the ideas of conservation and preservation high on their list. People who care about these issues are naturally inclined to want to make use of materials from the past around them in their homes and furniture.

Aesthetics

Surface texture, patina and the wood's core beauty distinguish reclaimed wood from new lumber. These unique attributes of tactility, patina, signs of age, rarity of grain and evidence of previous usage trigger our appreciation and make reclaimed wood precious.

Many are attracted to reclaimed wood because of what they see on its surface – its unadulterated raw appearance derived from the way it was originally processed, used and aged. They react to the wood's history with humanity. Others are mesmerized by the beauty of its core organic grain. Once milled, sanded and finished, Heritage Reclaimed woods afford a rare opportunity to go back in time and see the glory of primordial wood that can't be obtained today – unless it is from a reclaimed source.

Surface

Two of our most powerful senses are sight and touch, so when we are exposed to both sensations by the same object, our experience intensifies. No wonder so many people are attracted to the visual and tactile texture of reclaimed wood.

With furniture and some interior elements we have the unique opportunity to experience surfaces both visually and

Erica Diskin created this round table of Heritage Reclaimed longleaf pine for the Capo Restaurant in Boston. The wood shows much of the wear and blemishes from its original use.

through touch. Think about a coarse and weathered barn-wood wall that you can touch and appreciate. Imagine looking at the ceiling and noticing impressive timber beams scarred by hewing marks and nail holes, a testimony of their origin and the work that shaped them two centuries ago. Think about eating dinner on a table whose top was created from the thick floorboards of an industrial mill – checked, indented, perhaps even stained and riveted with pegs. After the boards are glued together, smoothed out and finished with moderation – just enough so that neither your shirt nor the linen would catch on the accented wood – your dining experience is enriched even more.

Rustic reclaimed lumber displays both surface patination and texture. This makes it great for additions to period-correct building or in projects that require complete reconstruction of buildings. Authentic posts and beams show the appropriate marks of a specific historical period. For example, if one wanted to build a new post-and-beam house that carries the hallmarks of rural 18th-century Colonial New England, they would probably look for reclaimed wood beams that were extracted from an old barn or house. The surface of these beams would look gray, brown or even black and show a scale-like pattern left by the surfacing tool chosen by the original carpenter who shaped the timber into posts and beams.

During the restoration of the historic Hartwell Tavern at Minute Man National Historical Park in Massachusetts, the crew made every effort to use appropriate reclaimed materials in roof, wall and floor repairs. For instance, boards used on the kitchen floor were those removed from the historic "Vose" House in Concord, Mass., when it was demolished in 1967.

Although not that old, this tool shed door is already showing the effects of exposure to the weather.

"Mushroom" wood.
EMILY DRYDEN

Surface texture

Surface texture is the physical evidence of the tools that shaped lumber, and testifies to the mechanical, biological and chemical forces, which over the years altered the landscape of the reclaimed wood. Was the original lumber hewed by an axe or an adze? Was it sawn by a pre-Industrial Revolution water saw? Had it been walked upon in a barn and gotten depressed by the hoofs of horses and cows? More surface textures include compression marks left on water tank staves as a result of the bracing force applied on them by the metal hoops that held the tank together.

But reclaimed texture can also come from less forceful conditions. Many reclaimed sidings or cladding boards salvaged from the walls of buildings show rugged surfaces that resulted from gradual erosion of the wood by the elements; we often refer to it simply as "weathering." With the help of the sun (UV radiation), wind and rain, the soft earlywood tissue slowly erodes, leaving behind the pronounced lines and curves of the more resilient and dense latewood ridges.

What else impacts the texture? Holes and grooves left by insects, and even pitting and bruises that are silent reminiscence for past presence of hardware and fasteners that were once embedded in the wood and later extracted.

Perhaps the most fascinating reclaimed texture that I have seen is the result of an organic transformation of the wood surfaces by acid, bacteria and fungi in the dark and humid

Striking patina caused by rust deposits over weathered wood.

facilities where mushrooms are grown. Mushroom beds are typically constructed from hemlock, cedar or cypress planks and then filled with compost made from straw and poultry manure. Gradually, with the help of moisture the mushrooms lay roots in the compost and embed into the planks, slowly digesting the susceptible earlywood and leaving the latewood proud of the surface. Once the bed can no longer serve its purpose the wood is dismantled and discarded, unless it is reclaimed. After cleaning the board with a high pressure water jet or a wire brush an attractive surface is revealed, displaying a terrain of spectacular flaky ridges and deep serpentine arroyos that look as if taken from the topography of a great desert of the Southwest.

Patina

Patina is the color change of the surface of either raw or painted wood as a result of environmental conditions, oxidation and aging. Examples of patination in reclaimed wood can include graying of the surface resulting from prolonged exposure to sunlight; staining after repeated contact with rusted metal hardware (such as hoops around a water tank) or infiltration by fungi; discoloration by oils, solvents and chemicals, mainly on floorboard planks retrieved from factories and mills, and even wine and whisky stains in wood reclaimed from barrels. Patina can also be present in wood that had been painted and over the years flaked off, got darker or lighter, eroded, bruised, etc., and now displays a complex irregular yet intriguing skin.

A ruler laid on a cross section of old-growth pecky cypress lumber reveals how slow and dense its growth rate was. In just two inches of board thickness one can count almost a century of life.

Wood's core beauty – the grain

Where in many cases we covet reclaimed wood for its opaque, ragged, period-appropriate look, in other instances we may seek to harvest what lay underneath its surface in order to expose, then celebrate, the splendor of the wood's color and grain, or what I call its "core."

A voyage back in time (or, trees are like time capsules)

Perhaps the most coveted characteristic of reclaimed wood core is its grain pattern. The grain is a manifestation of the tree's botanical characteristics (its DNA) and is a testimony to the environment it grew in and its age. As trees grow taller and wider, they enlarge their trunk circumference with sequential layers of new growth – layers of tissue added year by year and growth season by growth season. A rainy season, such as in the spring, will yield a wider and less-dense growth tissue, while a drier season, such as the summer, will generate a slower and denser tissue growth. In most cases a tree adds two new growth tissues per year. However, in warm tropical areas where it rains more frequently, the tree tissues grow constantly and thus the differences between the annual rings can sometimes be harder to identify and the texture of the grain is more homogenous.

Why is old-growth reclaimed wood so attractive?

Reclaimed lumber of significant heritage is often sought after for its core beauty. A good example is the heartwood of longleaf pine (also known as "heart pine"), from trees that originated in an old-growth forest. This softwood lumber is darker, denser and has tighter grain orientation than newly grown commercial longleaf pine. Old-growth pine that has vertical grain with 30 or even 50 grains per inch is cherished because the tree it came from slowly grew straight up in a virgin forest, getting higher and denser year by year for hundreds of years until it was cut down a century or two ago.

In a way, wood is like a vintage red wine or whisky where the longer it is allowed to age, the better it becomes. Con-

The author's "Etrog Box" was built mainly from reclaimed longleaf pine. Notice the tight parallel grain, a hallmark of a quartersawn Heritage Reclaimed wood.

trary to old-growth lumber, newer lumber such as Southern yellow pine – which is, in fact, longleaf pine – is a product of younger trees that grew fast in managed forests. Because of the rapid growing rate of younger trees, each growth tissue is wider. When the tree is harvested, which is much earlier than in bygone years, and is turned into lumber, its grain strips look broader and paler.

Another type of reclaimed softwood that is cherished for its beauty is Douglas fir. High-grade Douglas fir was a construction wood of choice by carpenters for hundreds of years. Before the 1920s, tight-grain Douglas fir was used both for the construction of houses and for building windows and doors. But by the 1940s and '50s demand for new housing skyrocketed, and high-grade lumber became scarcer. Suppliers began channeling the highest grade of lumber to the window and door manufacturers (who could not compromise on quality and needed dense, straight-grained lumber) while lower grade lumber, as long as it was structurally sound, was sold to carpenters as framing lumber.

Today it is almost impossible for anyone to buy new lumber that matches the quality and appeal of old-growth lumber. So if one wanted to replace old windows with new ones that look and feel as genuine as possible, or if a contractor is asked to repair flooring or add floorboards to an old building that should look period-correct, there is no other source but reclaimed lumber to provide that kind of level of authenticity.

Not all cores look alike

Cores of wood reclaimed from factories and mills will often be afflicted by checking, screw holes and nail holes, stains and other imperfections common to lumber that has been used and abused. Yet this is not the case with cores emerging from sinker logs or water-, vinegar- and brewing tanks where the wood was originally meticulously sorted to be of the highest grade and then, especially in the case of wine and hard liquor barrels, was kept in ideal conditions.

Possibly the best way to get a perfect period-correct match for old flooring is to use old flooring. Floorboards are among the most common reclaimed lumber.

Esteem

Esteem is the associated value, which is both emotional and concert, which we attribute to reclaimed wood. This reverence sometimes stems from the lumber's "biography" or provenance: where the tree came from, what function it served, what location it spent its service life in. Often we hold reclaimed wood in high esteem regardless of what it looks like. The story behind the wood or that it conveys becomes what is most important. Reclaimed wood from an old barn or tropical wood planks once used to pave the Coney Island boardwalk will rank high in esteem, while wood reclaimed from a recently built shipping pallet will rank lower.

Sometimes it is fantasy and nostalgia that drives up attributed value – an elusive tale that the wood "whispers to us" or the tale told by lumberyard folks, interior decorators or woodworkers who impart the wood's backstory. Perhaps the most potent potion that drives esteem is sentimentality and a yearning for authenticity; the conviction that by making use of reclaimed wood one gets closer to nature, to a specific historical time, or connects in a metaphysical way to the original people and values that created, and then made use, of that specific wood. The reclaimed wood has the magical ability to channel an era, a culture or a feeling from the past to our present day.

Economy

Many gravitate toward reclaimed wood hoping they can get it free of charge, or at a lesser cost, than new lumber. This is mostly true with Common Reclaimed wood from the side of the road, wood repurposed from found furniture, reclaimed wood obtained from Dumpster diving, lumber that has been given to us for free, or cutoff pieces from bigger projects that we recycle and re-use. But when comparing the board foot price of Heritage Reclaimed wood (of most species) to that of new wood bought at a specialized lumberyard, we often see that reclaimed wood is more expensive. This is because, although the lumberyard pays less per board foot of reclaimed wood than it would pay for new wood purchased from the mill, it needs to levy the high costs of initiating the reclaimed wood such as hardware extraction, resawing and drying – which, in many cases, is a labor-intensive process that ends up increasing the price.

That said, there is a way to buy Heritage Reclaimed wood and pay less. For this, one needs to commit to do much of the legwork that the professional reclaimers do. First you need to locate a source for buying or getting the lumber, then you need to arrange for it to be delivered and, lastly, carve out the time to process it yourself. I talk in length about the ways to obtain reclaimed wood for free in Chapter Three.

Live Oak Resurrection

Few doubt that the Southern live oak gave both valor and strength during America's infancy, not only as a symbol but also as an essential material for the building of the ships needed to ensure a young country's independence. But there's a story about this fabulous building material interwoven with American history, maritime technology and, of course, reclaim beauty that you've probably never heard. It is the story of massive Southern live oak logs that were stockpiled long ago, became forgotten and have miraculously been rediscovered.

Well over two centuries ago, the young republic resolved to build six state-of-the-art heavy frigates for the fledgling U.S. Navy. The prime wood, coveted for its strength and an innate natural curvature perfect for the geometry of a ship's framing, was native to the southern coast of the United States. Live oak trees don't grow tall and straight like the more common white or red oaks of cooler climates. Instead, they send out massive limbs horizontally from the trunk. The curvy trunks and limbs where a perfect fit for the construction of sailing ships, as the natural curves could be incorporated with little shaping into a ship's hull.

Live oak wasn't cherished just for a sublime accident of botanical geometry, but for its proven strength and rot resistance. The wood's reputation for toughness was gloriously reaffirmed in the War of 1812 when the U.S.S. *Constitution* (the Navy flagship at the time and one of the six heavy frigates) triumphed in naval battles against the British Royal Navy without significant damage. The ship's hull of live oak, built at the Charlestown Naval Yard in Boston and launched in 1797, easily repelled enemy shells and earned the ship the nickname "Old Ironsides."

The U.S.S. *Constitution*.

MARC A. POIRIER

Longleaf Lumber of Cambridge, Mass., is the prime source for Heritage live oak from the Charlestown Naval Yard. After initial cleaning, the timber can be sawn into boards, sliced into end grain plates or left as-is for mammoth projects requiring timbers.

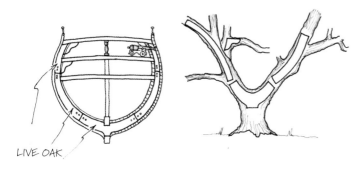

LIVE OAK

The reputation of live oak as a prime ship-building material skyrocketed, and by the beginning of the 19th century the shipyard decided to stock up on live oak. To have it ready as the need arose to expand the fleet, they cached the timber in a salt pond for long-term preservation. With the advent of iron and steel boat construction, however, the shipyard lost interest in its live oak stock and filled in the salt pond in the early 1900s.

Fast forward to 2010. By that time the Charlestown Naval Yard had become a National Historical Park and home base

to the restored U.S.S. Constitution, while the old salt pond was all but forgotten. That is, until the buried logs were uncovered during a construction project.

The timber was immaculately preserved, stained by soil and mud but otherwise in pristine condition. After its resurrection this timber has become an unprecedented historical Heritage Reclaim resource for use in both local and national carpentry, furniture and interior projects.

My friend Mitch Ryerson (you'll hear more about Mitch in Chapter Five) is one of only a few makers given the opportunity to work with America's most precious treasured wood, bestowing this timber with a new purpose as benches and other outdoor structures. Some of his creations, made from the timber that helped forge American independence, are installed at Cambridge Common. It's now a public park, but almost two hundred and fifty years ago was the field where General Washington, standing under an elm tree, assumed command of the Continental Army.

Ryerson made this live oak bench with a backrest of curved black locust.

▲ To enable the creation of very long benches, woodworker Mitch Ryerson connects two arched live oak timber beams with a traditional scarf joint.

Mitch Ryerson's live oak bench at a playground in Cambridge, Mass. ▶

CHAPTER 2

The Reclaimed Warehouse Experience
The world of large-scale reclaiming operations

Alan Solomon of Sawkill Lumber Co. runs one of the most prolific reclaim operations in the greater New York City area. Alan is a passionate reclaimer and a strong proponent of the Reuse, Repurpose and Recycle movement. I've know him for a few years now, ever since he invited me to participate in a reclaimed-wood furniture show that happened, of all places, on the street corner between 14th Street and 9th Avenue in Manhattan. During a visit to Sawkill and many conversations over the phone with him, I learned about new developments in one of the most exciting areas of the lumber industry. I am sure that this information will be of use to anyone who loves wood and reveres reclaimed materials.

Over the years Alan has gained unprecedented experience in locating reclaim resources, gathering the lumber, processing it and selling it. His clients include professional cabinetmakers, designers, makers, woodworkers and stage and art directors of the NYC bustling movie and theater industries. While Sawkill's modest showroom and warehouse is located in Brooklyn, N.Y., the bulk of their processing operations are run in rural New England by his business partner, Klaas Armster of Armster Reclaimed Lumber Company. Occasionally Alan will locate a source for reclaimed lumber in New York City, such as an old factory or a brownstone building that is to be torn down. But more often the lumber he resources comes from the East Coast, the Midwest and sometimes from overseas.

Just a small section of the lumberyard at Armster Reclaimed Lumber Co. in East Windsor, Conn., contains thousands of pieces of reclaimed stock.

Using reclaimed wood as a backdrop for high-end photography – here, for some delicious Santa Rosa plum cake with crème fraîche – is a popular trend.

Even the largest city can be a prime source of reclaimed lumber, like the immense beams in this about-to-be-gone old factory.

MARC A. POIRIER

Who buys reclaimed wood?

While finding reclaimed lumber on a small scale can surely be done by both amateurs and professional woodworkers, you will probably have to enlist the help of reclaim specialists in order to get a higher volume of lumber, or when exotic reclaims are what you (or your clients) require. With the greater demand for reclaimed wood, the industry that finds, processes and sells it is growing.

Today, near or within our big urban centers one can find a growing number of lumberyards and warehouses that specialize in reclaimed lumber. Some of those places were established many years ago but others showed up around the turn of the 21st century and the advent of the Maker Movement along with the growing demand for environmentally correct materials. The "Hipster-agrarian" look as well as "Homesteader decor" also generate demands for reclaimed wood. Interior designers, woodworkers, product photographers, and many times the end customers themselves, such as homeowners, find out about these places and pay a visit to look at their inventory.

EMILY DRYDEN

Most of the wood bought in reclaim centers is used for flooring, wall cladding and ceilings. Reclaimed lumber is often bought to serve as an authentic raw material in architectural millwork projects. It's also procured for the construction of buildings and interiors whose designers aim for an appropriate historical look. Furniture makers also purchase reclaimed wood.

As it happens, reclaimed wood isn't just used for building tangible long-lasting projects and objects. In recent years it has been an integral component in the image, marketing and entertainment industries too. Product and food photographs, set designers and catalog art directors ask for it. In this area the rustic nostalgic look of Heritage Reclaims trend the strongest.

Think about a sleek laptop computer photographed over a rugged reclaimed-wood desktop, or crystal-clear whisky glasses photographed on a rustic, weathered, reclaimed-wood tabletop mockup. In movies and theater sets, production designers incorporate it to suggest a period in time or evoke a

A SIGN FOR A GROUNDHOG

We are very fortunate to have cats, chickens and a toddler in our lives. In our garden and in the woodland behind it we occasionally see deer, squirrels, chipmunks, turkeys and many types of birds that either live in the woods or pass by, plus one more animal – a chubby groundhog we named Bennet, who made our garden his home.

Bennet pops up from time to time to eat the grass, flowers and the vegetables we grow. He set up shop in the old root base of what used to be a gigantic oak tree, which by now has been reduced to hardly anything but a few loosely formed root remains.

The old oak was surrounded by a mound of stones that, in my imagination, resembled a castle. I found some discarded citronella torches and staked them around the stones, telling our son Asher that these were the towers for Bennet's castle. After all this fairy tale buildup I felt that I had to make Bennet's domain official. I painted the name "Bennet" on a piece of reclaimed wood and hung it in front of the castle on a metal garden ornamental post that I found (yet again) in a neighbor's free-stuff pile.

Let's hope that our little woodchuck friend appreciates the effort.

The first step for processing reclaimed timber is to clean away years of paint, plaster, dirt and debris.

Rusted hardware extracted from reclaimed lumber fills up the barrels at Armster Reclaimed Lumber Company.

particular mood. They might not use the entire thickness of the reclaimed plank, and order it to be resawn into thin panels of 1/4" or even 1/8" thick veneer, then to be affixed onto a lightweight substrate of their liking. The marketing industry also makes use of reclaimed wood as promotional material containers, order boxes, trays and crates. Reclaimed wood is used for event organization to support a theme and as a visual identity enhancer.

Supply and demand influence the bulk of the reclaimed wood inventory, and much like the emerging farmers' market culture, their "in-stock" can vary greatly. Stock is often limited in size and quality and is dictated by the existing shape and condition of the repurposed lumber that the warehouse "hunter-gatherers" were able to find. On the flip side, the big reclaimed-wood distributors can offer slabs, planks, beams and columns of timber in mammoth sizes, extracted from century-old structures, that exceed the nominal sizes that regular lumber distributors can normally offer.

How professional reclaimers process wood

Most professional reclaimers begin processing reclaimed timber by brushing off debris using a stiff brush, compressed air or even water pressure. Then with the help of a metal detector they will inspect for hardware that may be embedded in the wood, such as nails, screws, hinges, brackets, etc. Once they identify these contaminates they meticulously extract them.

After this they have two options: First, they can offer the wood for sale in its raw state. This means preserving its original dimensions and any surface character such as paint and patina. In this case they will probably pass it through a kiln to regulate the moisture content, but also to eliminate any bug infestations.

The other option is to resaw the lumber into planks to expose the core wood, and then kiln dry the planks. If the wood is painted they will most likely skin the wood on a lumber mill-style band saw to get rid of layers of paints and other

Armster uses this large Wood-Mizer sawmill – a portable large-scale band saw – for resawing reclaimed wood.

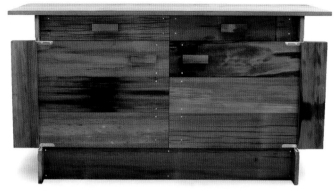

Piet Hein Eek's "Water Tower Dresser" is made from redwood salvaged from water towers torn down in New York City. Although planed, the wood still shows the discoloration and stresses from its years in service.

Stacks of reclaimed lumber and resawn reclaimed planks inside the kiln at Armster. Often, reclaimed wood posts and beams from mill buildings, bridges and other massive structures, as well as reclaimed logs used as barn sleeper joists, are resawn and then kiln-dried to ensure compatibility with modern woodworking needs and to guarantee complete eradication of wood-burrowing insects.

surface characteristics prior to resawing it into planks.

In cases of reclaimed siding, floor planks and other thinner boards, the reclaim warehouses often tend to surface the underside of the planks on a jointer, planer or belt sander followed by a short stint in the kiln. Special reclaims such as mushroom growing bed boards whose surface is exceptionally grooved, pitted or distorted, and have accumulated dirt and organic material, will receive a "facial cleansing" via pressure-washing equipment, followed by a short stay in the kiln.

The lumber may receive only slight amounts of processing where planks and boards are "skip-planed," a technique of lightly surfacing rough reclaimed wood with the intention to leave some of the original texturing and patina behind. Done by planing or sanding, the outcome is a partially smoothed surface plateau, with coarser original sawn or weathered wood in patches and valleys.

Large-scale reclaimed timber is placed on the bed of the mill and then resawn into planks, which liberates century-old lumber and exposes splendid grain, structure and color. After the resawing is completed the new/old lumber is placed in the kiln. Armster uses a kiln to expedite the removal of "free water" from the lumber. Since the lumber has already lost its inner cells' water (bound water) many years ago, either through natural drying or air drying, not much kiln energy is needed for the drying process. Armster just needs to heat the lumber to make sure that any water that penetrated the grain as a result of rain or high moisture levels during shipping or outdoor storage will be removed. This surplus moisture is called free water.

The reclaim warehouse "Field Guide"

Here are just a few highlights from the vast and exciting varieties of reclaimed wood found at a typical reclaimed lumber dealer.

Old growth longleaf pine, commonly referred to as heart pine

Heart pine's beauty comes from its remarkable age and growth history. It is a spectacular wood to work with as it is rich in color and contrast, and is priced for its structural density and radiant charm. Originally harvested from old-growth trees it is now sourced from dismantled structural elements such as posts, beams, sleepers and floorboards extracted from mill buildings, barns and old houses.

A ruler shows the exceptionally tight grain of old-growth heart pine. Wide growth rings show when the tree had a prosperous growth season, while tighter rings indicate tougher conditions that slowed down its growth.

Old-growth tank staves

Used for vinegar, wine or pickle tanks. Tank staves are important resources for reclaimed wood. Sometimes their provenance and story is even more interesting than their appearance. Such is the case with Worcestershire sauce tank wood. This historic tank was in the original Manhattan-based factory of the American subsidiary of Lea & Perrins brand until the 1950s, when the company dismantled the tank and moved it to New Jersey. In 2015 the company retired the tank and Armster Reclaimed Lumber harvested its timber staves, which were amazing old-growth Douglas fir.

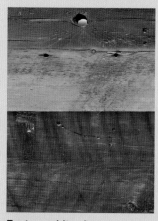

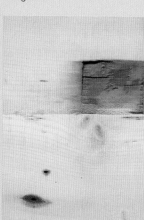

Pecky cypress floor joists

An interesting variety of cypress lumber that displays numerous, odd-shaped cavities caused by fungi when the tree was still alive. The pecky appearance is limited to the heartwood.

Eastern white pine

Milled from the tallest trees of the Northeastern forests, Eastern white pine played a critical role in American life and history. It was the most versatile and widely used wood of the Colonial era up until the mid-1800s. Reclaimed Eastern white pine boards provide for exceptionally wide planks and today are repurposed into floors, paneling and other applications within the scope of both modern and traditional design. Reclaimed planks often present nail holes, indentation, stress cracks and other character marks which allow them to maintain both unique and unifying looks across every board of this splendid wood. Eastern white pine is sold in two main categories: **Pumpkin pine** (above left) is cleaner and clearer looking, contains fewer nail holes and appears darker with distinct cinnamon golden tones. **Rustic white pine** (above right) is lighter, contains more knots, nail holes, checking and other imperfections that present diverse visual elements of character and use.

Redwood from water, wine or container tanks

Unplaned redwood staves reclaimed from water tanks show a "corduroy" pattern on their exterior as a result of years of earlywood grain erosion. The lumber is also lined with depression marks, left by the steel bands or hoops that held the tank together. Both the thin corduroy strips and the depression marks make this wood's patinated surface very beautiful. The structural integrity of water tank wood can be somewhat compromised by the chlorine in drinking water, which damages the wood over time. Therefore, it's important to test the wood for strength before buying it for a demanding project. When the tank staves are resawn the outcome is a vivid red-pink tight and straight-grained wood that may include sporadic areas of grayish black cloud-like patches.

Mushroom growing bed lumber

Mushrooms need a natural substance to grow on, and hemlock or cypress wood planks have been reliably used for building mushroom beds. The beds are filled with compost made from straw and manure. Over time the enzymes in the organic matter digest and erode the surface of the planks, consume the softer wood tissues and leave behind a most spectacular sculptural topography of latewood. Mushroom-bed wood is routinely replaced when the planks become too fragile, so it is an excellent and consistent source of reclaimed wood.

HARDWOODS

Chestnut

Valued for its beautiful warm tones, contrasting earlywood vs. latewood grain, and delightful milling qualities, American chestnut was once a prime timber coveted by many. Tragically, this specie was eradicated by blight in the early 20th century. Reclaimed old barn structures and timber from demolished mill buildings are perhaps the sole source for chestnut, making it among the rarest of reclaimed woods.

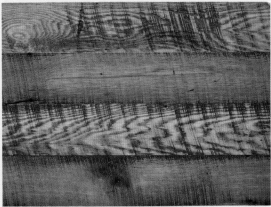

EMILY DRYDEN

Barn oak

This wood is mostly salvaged from rural structures – barns, horse fences and storage tanks. Light brown with darker highlights, barn oak is known for its even-grained hardwood with a range of character marks that include sound stress cracks, small knots and nail holes — which distinguish this type of reclaimed from freshly cut oak. With its durability, varied grain, warm color tones and workability, along with the character marks of its history, barn oak is among the most popular reclaimed wood species. Skip-planed barn oak (above) can be of true provenance, or be induced by processing fully weathered planks via sanding or shaving off part of the patinated terrain.

Wormy timber

This is lumber that was "visited" by beetle larva and as a result shows unique hole patterns.

Boardwalk angelique

From Coney Island, Atlantic City or Far Rockaway boardwalks damaged when hurricane Sandy hit the shores of Long Island and New Jersey. Many of the boardwalks there had to be rebuilt while the old lumber, almost all of it made from angelique and other exotics with amazing rot-resistant qualities, has been reclaimed and is now offered for sale in both surfaced (above) and weathered varieties (below).

"Mudcrack Lumber"

Formed as a result of moisture-rotted surface that has dried and hardened again without penetrating too deeply into the core wood. You'll find this variety in both hardwood and softwood species.

Dunnage wood

Dunnage wood comes in different shapes and forms; from massive beams to small 3"-square batons. It is used to separate and cushion between heavy equipment elements during shipment, separate massive shipping containers on cargo ships, and as a dampening material to space apart railroad tracks. Shipped from Japan (but harvested in Malaysia or Indonesia), it's instrumental in lashing down equipment on the move. On the outside this lumber looks gray or black and in this raw state may be suitable for projects that demand a rustic look. But once resawn, it reveals the rich grain of tropical hardwood. Some types of lumber used for dunnage are known also as "Japanese Box Wood"

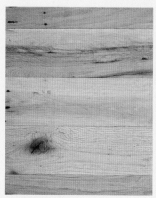

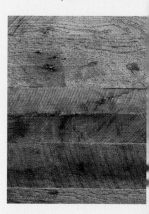

Cargo wood

This wood is mostly obtained from shipping containers and dismantled equipment crates and hardwood pallets. It can be surfaced (as the cargo oak above left) or in its natural, weathered state (cargo oak, above right).

Red barn siding

Red barn siding from iconic American farm buildings evokes warmth, vibrancy and nostalgia. To protect their buildings' sidings, farmers used orange-colored linseed oil mixed with milk, lime and iron oxide (rust) to make their paint reddish-brown and render it mold- and moss-resistant. The color and texture range of red barn siding is rather wide, with weathered gray or brown board beneath, and inconsistent paint coverage and surface dynamics. These reclaimed boards are interspersed with nail holes, knots, checks and varying levels of faded paints and come in both hardwood and softwood varieties.

BARN AND HOMESTEAD TIMBER

Pioneers and farmers built their homes and barns by sourcing lumber on site, felling trees at and around the location where the buildings were to stand. They sawed and hewed the logs into timber and used it to erect the structure. They couldn't be too picky and used whatever log materials they could find. Therefore, we often see a variety of tree species comprising the various structural components of early rural buildings and barns. Under the same roof it's common to find oak, pine, spruce, fir, hemlock, beech and birch, and often even fruit trees, plus a few species that are now almost extinct such as chestnut, elm and ash.

Although flat top and bottom, these beams are still partially rounded.

Hewing a log.

From top: Unprocessed log; hand-hewn log; sawn log.

Texture and patina

Reclaimed wood of character and beauty is defined by its history, surface augmentation, core beauty or a combination of all three. The surface is the most recognized quality of reclaimed wood. It can emerge from the way the timber was initially processed. Logs may be hewn, sawn, or riven – all are ways of transforming logs into beams, slabs and boards, and can be done by hand labor or with the help of mechanized devices. Each method can yield an interesting surface texture. But surface identity can also emanate from the way a wood has aged and has been exposed to weather, insects, paint, foot traffic and chemicals.

Texture as a result of lumber processing

Some basic historic structures were made of logs that had hardly been processed. Those logs, used as sills, posts, girts, beams, joists and other elements, retained their roundish tree trunk shape, and even traces of bark.

Hewn and sawn timber

A step up from this rustic look included logs that were roughly shaped with tools such as broadaxes and adzes to impose flat facets and squarish proportions on them. The trees were felled, and a carpenter would chip away their exterior to flatten the rounded trunk, persistently chopping the bark and sapwood to shape two or four long facets. This technique of flattening and truing the sides is called hand-hewing. Hand-hewn reclaimed timber has a scaly surface shaped by the geometry of the blade tools and the upper-body swing technique that formed it hundreds of years ago.

As more resources and workers became available, improvements were made in the ways trees were processed into building elements. Once you had two people on site, logs could be sawn into slabs, boards and beams in a saw pit. Sawing produced smoother and flatter timber, thanks to the consistency and dependability of the sawing rhythm.

If a brook was flowing nearby, a watermill could have

Hewing marks on a reclaimed post.

The beam whose surface shows parallel strips (top) was probably sawn with a water mill or a commercial band saw. The one with the arced strips (above) was cut on a circular mill saw.

been established and a water-powered saw could expedite and improve both productivity and consistency of the produced timber. Pit-sawn and water-milled timber show straighter saw marks that vary in width on the surface of the timber. In the first quarter of the 19th century a way to cut logs via a circular saw was invented. If the side of a reclaimed wood beam shows a pattern of moderate arches, it was probably milled with a circular saw.

Planed surface

Many Heritage Reclaimed boards, particularly vintage floorboards and interior sidings were originally surfaced by a handplane – a manual tool used for shaping and smoothing wooden surfaces. Depending on the job requirements and the skill of the woodworker, planed surfaces show ridges and valleys, undulations, tear-out and other surface augmentation that attest to the random nature of handwork. Even so, planed surfaces are much smoother than hand-hewn surfaces.

Handplaning for a smooth surface.

About 25 years ago I built for my mother a shed for her garden tools that included reclaimed oak doors made from dismantled pallets. After building the doors I finished them with a few coats of spar varnish. Over the years sun and rain challenged the finish and the wood underneath. Areas of wood protected by the roof of the shed or by the horizontal or diagonal cross rails managed to retain some of the varnish, and the wood underneath it still looks dark brown. Below that area where the wood was less protected the varnish eroded and the exposed wood fibers turned light gray. And in areas where the wood received the highest volume of sun radiation and water, its surface became dark gray.

Texture and patina as a result of the elements

When bare wood is exposed to occasional water from rain and snow, and light radiation from the sun, it will eventually turn gray, crack and potentially cup. The sun's UV radiation causes photochemical degradation, which is responsible for the decomposition of the lignin in wood cells. As the lignin is destroyed, the outer fiber layer of the wood is weakened and turns gray. As the cells are subjected to more damage, and expand and contract with moisture, the boards themselves will deform and check.

Some species of wood, such as teak, mahogany, white oak, ipe, cedar, redwood and black locust are very resilient to weathering and decay. If untreated with a wood finish their outer layer will eventually turn gray, but this grayness is only on the surface, and once removed we are able to access pristine wood. Most other wood species are influenced by rain and sun in a more profound way. But from experience I can attest that with a minimal amount of surface removal even the most inexpensive and common lumber can be brought back to life and serve magnanimously in your new project, as long as it is not rotting from within.

One caveat: Since weathering is one of the most unique attributes of reclaimed wood, in many cases we would intentionally want to preserve and celebrate it in the new piece.

Wood erosion

Shingles, siding, floors, and other exterior elements made of wood are subjected to erosion. Wind batters the wood with dust, sand and pieces of branches and leaves. Rain inflicts upon the lumber acidity and minerals. Houses built by the sea endure a constant barrage of saltwater and sand that erodes and scars their surface, ages and blisters the wood with unique character and texture. Erosion works its "magic" on finished wood, too. It scratches and peels paint and varnish, and like a great abstract artist gives wood sidings, doors, shades and other painted surfaces remarkable textures and accents.

Natural wood surfaces do not erode homogeneously. The softer earlywood erodes faster and deeper than the latewood. This is why we see, especially in exposed wooden surfaces, a pattern of high and low lines. It is exceptionally visible in the exterior of heritage redwood or cedar water tank staves made from trees that grow slowly for hundreds of years. The tightness of the seasonal growth manifests on the staves' surface in the shape of hairline-width parallel gray ridges and valleys, which make this reclaimed wood quite spectacular.

Shopping reclaimed wood – the walk-in experience

A visit to a reclaimed-wood warehouse, or yard, is a unique experience. You may have an idea of what you're looking for and hope you'll be able to find it, but that might change the moment you see the overwhelming reclaim options available. In many reclaim warehouses you'll find yourself surrounded by an endless bounty of wood and timber in different shapes, conditions, patination, species and sizes. While some facilities are better organized than others and offer sorted stacks, bins and shelves, upon which nicely

This beautiful piece of driftwood salvaged by the author from the Hudson River Estuary shows the effects of years of erosion.

Reclaimed wood from an old barn was used to build a sleeping loft and other interior elements in this New York City apartment. The owner that commissioned the loft had fond memories of the family barn where he spent much of his childhood, and wanted to create a homage to his past experiences via the use of similar materials. (Loft owners: Dhinesh N Muthu and Jonathan Blackford; designer: Jacob Perkins)

labeled lumber lay in an orderly manner just waiting to be plucked out and catch a ride back home with you, other outlets can be messy, dusty and disorganized.

Reclaimed wood prices vary depending mainly on a couple of factors, including the amount of resources and time needed to prepare the lumber, and the rarity and the demand for wood itself. Prices for Heritage Reclaimed wood are sometimes 20% to 40% higher than for new lumber of the same species.

In order to make your visit productive you should exercise patience and be prepared to endure dust, cold, heat, sun and rain. Since most of these outlets – and I have visited many over the years – may be geared toward professional high-volume buyers, you also need to take into account that the people who service you may not have the appetite to attend to the "single-board" buyer. If you only want to buy a small quantity of wood, begin by checking the warehouse's website to see if it describes itself as friendly toward amateur woodworkers and others who buy in small quantities. Give them a call in advance and ask when is the best time to come over.

Bring a pair of gloves, a tape measure, a pencil and something to write on. A block plane to help you shave off patina and expose the true grain and color of the lumber is also a

good companion. You also want to ask if the wood you're buying is moisture- and insect-free. As noted earlier, most reclaim warehouses process their wood in a kiln to get rid of extra moisture and wood-burrowing insects, but you should make sure this is the case with the lumber you fancy to buy. These small steps will facilitate a stress-free and productive visit for both you and the reclaim warehouse employees.

Goodwin River Recovered Lumber

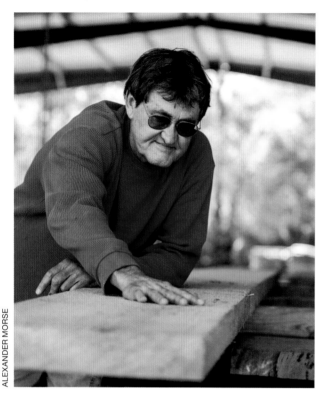

ALEXANDER MORSE

George Goodwin inspects planks in his inventory.

Goodwin Company – Fine Antique Wood Since 1976
The Original River Recovered® Specialists
Log Boom on the Suwannee River, circa 1875

This section of an old stereo-viewer card shows an 1875 image of logs being floated down the Suwannee River, not far from the Goodwin Company's home base in Micanopy, Fla.

"I feel good about what I am doing," says George Goodwin in Rex Jones' documentary *Longleaf: The Heart of Heart Pine.* "You know, I feel very positive for not cutting trees, and instead being involved in recycling something that is valuable and beautiful, and basically rescue it from never being seen, enjoyed and appreciated."

Goodwin is one of the founding fathers of the re-claimed-lumber industry and the person who coined and trademarked the term "River-Recovered." Together with his wife, Carol, Goodwin established one of the most prolific reclaimed-wood enterprises in the world. Their specialty is re-covering underwater logs that sank to the bottom of rivers in the Southeastern part of the U.S., especially in the company's home state of Florida.

These logs, mainly of longleaf pine and bald cypress trees

that were cut down throughout the 19th and the early 20th centuries, were floated down rivers toward sawmills and seaports. A percentage of these old-growth trees, however, sank on the way to the mill and were forgotten.

In the 1970s he came up with the idea of hoisting the logs, resawing and selling their precious core lumber to any-body who appreciates the rarity and beauty of centuries-old timber. Many of the logs the Goodwin Company recovers come from trees that germinated more than a thousand years ago, then matured and aged slowly for hundreds of years only to be cut down in the late 19th and early 20th centuries. The richness of color, grain pattern and impres-sive structural integrity in these old-timers is unprecedented and make them a coveted Heritage resource.

When customers approach the Goodwins to buy lumber

This intricate marquetry in the floor of a private home, crafted with River-Recovered heart pine and cypress, received a 2008 "Floor of the Year" award from the National Wood Flooring Assoc.

The ceiling at the University of Florida Hawkins Center at Farrior Hall is made entirely of Goodwin's River-Recovered heart pine.

it's not enough to say you want to purchase Heritage heart pine. You'll need to be specific about what kind of heart pine, as their catalog has an impressive number of subcategories for this wonderful material. And the same goes for the bald cypress lumber, which is another magnificent specimen that used to cover much of the Southeast. Here are a few highlights from their collection of heart pine:

- **Clear** – Displays cathedral arches with graceful grain movement.
- **Vertical** – A more formal, sometimes modern look with tight, striped graining
- **Midnight** – Chocolate, cherry tones appearing older than most antique heart pine. Goodwin's original antique River-Recovered midnight heart pine stock came from the mysterious waters of the Savannah River. These woods withstood the elements and show shades of dark blue and gray.
- **Curly** – Which is, by the way, one of my favorite woods. Its figure is like no other burl wood in the world. Antique River-Recovered curly heart pine is extremely rare. It is an amazing wood that never fails to turn heads. Often found only in the outer board of one out of every 400 or so River-Recovered logs. Also known as rosemary or burly heart pine.

The pecky cypress used for this ceiling makes for a stunning display.

The Goodwin's antique River-Recovered cypress lumber is as interesting as their heart pine collection. Recovered cypress is used more in walls, doors, ceilings and paneling and less as a flooring material, which is the main domain of the heart pine. One of the most striking types of cypress the Goodwins carry is called "pecky" cypress. It got its look as a result of inner fungus activity that occurred when the tree was still alive. The fungi created a matrix of narrow, elongated eye-shaped voids along the trunk. As the logs are milled the cavities appear on the board surfaces with an appearance like woven wood lace.

CHAPTER 3

A Reclaim Resource Guide

Finding reclaimed wood and other materials
for free (or for little money)

Throughout most of my life I have collected all kinds of useful items for my woodworking – from the sides of roads, from Dumpsters near the loading docks of warehouses and factories, from the grounds of lumber mills, and even from bins of "firewood" scraps discarded in the studios I apprenticed in. Over the 20 years that I've been a serious woodworker, my skills as a hunter-gatherer of reclaimed materials evolved and improved to the point that I feel confidant sharing with you what I know. In this chapter I'll reveal the most inexpensive and fruitful ways to obtain reclaimed wood and hardware, and lay out some proven techniques to process and initiate these materials for your projects.

Your best bet for finding reclaimed wood is through word of mouth, "Freecycling" websites, Craigslist, woodworking forums, social media, local online or old-fashioned classifieds boards, and simply by spotting it with your own eyes.

The amount of free materials available to us is vast, from Heritage Reclaimed to Common Reclaimed and from salvaged timber to scrap wood. But for us to succeed in finding and gathering these materials we have to get one major inhibition that every healthy human being possesses under control. Yes, I'm talking about shame and embarrassment.

Almost everyone feels uncomfortable with the thought of stopping near a pile of free stuff and sorting through it. We feel embarrassed and don't want anyone passing by to notice. More than anything, we don't want the original owner of the items – a neighbor, perhaps – wondering if our life turned for the worst to the point that we have to sort through their old stuff. We fear being stigmatized as hoarders, poor or even homeless.

Another potential source for inconvenience is replying to

A fruitful foraging expedition can turn up everything from old beams to furniture parts.

◀ The author looks for usable wood and other materials in a Dumpster at Harvard University.

Moving day is a perfect time to find old furniture and usable materials that don't make it into the moving van.

Free wood (and stuff) in your own neighborhood: when, what and how

Perhaps the easiest available option to gather free reclaimed wood, hardware, glass and other useful tools and equipment that will enhance your work environment and projects, is to pay attention to your immediate surroundings. By that I mean to open your eyes wide as you walk down the street, drive or cycle. The stuff your neighbors dispose of could be your best resource – the only thing you need is courage. Here are a few tips and suggestions.

- Find out in what evenings your neighbors and those who live nearby put out their trash; this is the best time for you to make your rounds and spot goodies.

- Make note of when people in your area tend to clean out basements, garages and sheds (typically in the spring). This is an excellent time to hunt for leftover plywood, unwanted furniture and discarded tools.

- Spot "House for Sale" signs and make a mental note to pass by occasionally. As sellers double their efforts to fix up their homes and prepare for moving, often they'll aggressively go through, and get rid of, unwanted belongings.

- Seek out houses, factories, workshops and school buildings in your area that are scheduled for intense renovation or demolition. Contractors, developers and owners may hire professional reclaimers to maximize every drop of value from the property, but there's almost always something left behind after the professional reclaimers take the prime wood. Obviously, you don't want to get into legal trouble, so do not trespass. Instead, try to visit the site when workers are there, and politely ask to talk to the foreperson of the demolition or the reclaiming crew. Inquire if there are any discarded materials that you might save. In many cases you won't leave empty-handed. Most professional reclaimers are looking for prime Heritage reclaims, for posts and beams of maximum size and minimal defects. While these prime materials will be extracted, wood of lesser quality – to them – may be left behind. It's not economical for many professional reclaimers to deal with smaller, deformed or split boards riddled with nails or bolts. However, if you're willing to put in the time to clean and prepare those discarded materials, you may end up with some great material for your next project.

and negotiating with a stranger who posted an ad for free or inexpensive reclaimed lumber. Most of us are used to shopping for materials in stores or online, and feel secure knowing that the prices are fixed and that the institutions we buy from are professional. Anything that veers away from our comfort zone can feel unfamiliar and threatening.

But, my dear reader, I have to tell you that one of the most effective ways to get reclaimed materials for free is to push out of your comfort zone, roll up your sleeves, swallow your pride and dive into the stuff on the side of the road or at the sweet ending of a Craigslist "free stuff" ad.

▲ A realtor's "for sale" sign often goes hand-in-hand with free materials and wooden items.

After professional reclaimers have gotten all the best wood, there may still be usable items. Designer Piet Hein Eek turned discarded windows into an attractive display case ▶

General recommendations

In woodworking and carpentry forums, on Craigslist and the like, individuals and companies offer reclaimed wood for sale via ads and word of mouth. This wood is often described as "barn wood" or "industrial timber for sale," but if you're really lucky it might even be donated for free.

Begin by examining the pictures provided by the seller or donor and contact them in order to obtain as much information about the wood before you commit to visiting them. Some owners/sellers may not want to spend much time with back-and-forth emails or text messages, so offer to call them. If possible, be willing to go look at the wood but don't commit to buy until you're comfortable with the quality of the wood and the price. You don't want to give the seller false hope, nor do you want to regret a hasty purchase.

In many cases the price will be very reasonable, as the seller naturally expects you, the buyer, to deal with all cleanup of the wood. Be ready to extract fasteners, dry the wood, remove dirt and paint and possibly eradicate pests. There is also a possibility that the reclaimed lumber may be offered free of charge. There are many generous people still around who might not want money for their barn timber or sidings that unfortunately just collapsed. You might find someone who's simply grateful for you to clear the debris from their property, in which case both parties come out winners. Don't expect sellers to provide loading help, as they may be elderly, disabled or just unable to assist. Make whatever arrangements you need to haul the wood and make sure to bring tools (and, possibly, a companion) to help you with this task.

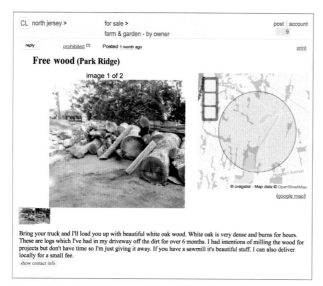

A typical Craigslist ad. Here is one for free white oak logs.

Most shipping pallets are made from softwood and are easy to find at the loading areas of businesses, supermarkets, factories, etc. Sometimes, however, you can find hardwood pallets, like these oak pallets given for free via Craigslist.

MAHOGANY IN DISGUISE

Please don't be deceived by the monochromatic look of weathered gray-green furniture. What lies beneath the surface can be a completely different story. After saving this table from the Dumpster I looked closely at the grain pattern on the very wide solid top. At first I thought it might be walnut, but after a few strokes with a fine-tuned plane, the beauty of mahogany revealed itself. This table's legs are also made of solid, rot-resistant mahogany that stood up well to the elements.

Craigslist (www.craigslist.org)

Begun as a local email distribution list to friends in the San Francisco area in 1995, Craigslist is now the most recognized website for posting free classified ads. Craigslist provides individuals and businesses the ability to offer an abundance of items for sale or for free pick up, from whole barns to a box of rusty nails to a forlorn rubber ducky. Craigslist is now available in more than 70 countries and in different languages. It includes classic categories such as furniture, toys, tools, and cars for sale, but also many specialized categories, including one of my favorites: "Free Stuff."

Craigslist is a great place to buy reclaimed wood, reclaimed glass and sometimes reclaimed hardware. You'll find fallen trees, logs, billets (short logs) and branches, pallet wood and barn wood on the site. The pallets are mostly free, and so are fallen trees and much of the firewood billets. In most cases you can just come and pick them up, as the current owner wants rid of them. If your furniture project demands glass components such as doors or shelves, you should definitely check Craigslist ads, as people routinely get rid of old windows, glass shelves and framed artwork which you can take apart and utilize the glass panels.

This old gristmill in Meyersdale, Pa., will be a treasure trove of barn wood once reclaimed.

Barn wood

Barn wood and any other Heritage Reclaimed wood is a different story, as the owner might be well aware of the apparent value of reclaimed barn wood. It is likely that they're trying to sell the wood rather than give it away for free. The price per board foot varies quite dramatically and depends on the type of lumber offered, its condition, the location and age of the barn, and how badly the sellers want to get rid of it.

Barn wood for sale can emerge from a recently collapsed barn, typically due to age, neglect or storm damage. Barns are also torn down due to economic necessities of repurposing the land for a development project, or because the owners need to erect a newer, more modern barn in place of the old one.

In all these cases the landowner may want to sell the wood rather than deal with the hassle of disposing it, which is a costly process. But also remember that many barn owners are farmers trying to make ends meet, and really need the money from the sale of their old barn timber and wood.

Still, there are many occasions when barn wood might be offered for free. From time to time you will see an ad declaring "free barn wood." This wood might be the leftovers from the sale of the more lucrative barn lumber that was procured by professional reclaimers. Yet even if this wood has lain outside and deteriorated, parts of it can still be salvaged and brought back to life. If you're willing to invest a little time and gas you just might find some nice lumber there.

Free wood scraps

Another type of reclaimed wood available through Craigslist is scrap lumber, or even new hardwood and softwood stock being discarded by its owners due to a move or a family/personal circumstance. These kinds of Craigslist ads may specify free lumber or free scraps. And while technically this wood may not be considered by some as actually reclaimed, since it wasn't previously used or salvaged, I include it under the reclaim umbrella. Don't forget that if not for us like-minded wood enthusiasts this lumber would have ended up in the landfill.

The main contributors to the free scraps or free lumber Craigslist offerings sometimes include woodworkers who need to move and face the reality of deciding what to take with them and what to leave behind, or conscientious family members or caregivers of elderly, ill or deceased woodworkers who are consolidating a loved one's shop. These good people have probably tried to sell or donate tools and machinery, and after most of the valuable shop possessions are given away, are left with miscellaneous pieces of wood.

Be patient and empathic when paying a visit to the home of a retired or deceased woodworker. Keep in mind a lifetime's wood inventory and perhaps other items are being given away. Be open to listening to stories about past projects and anecdotes, and even offer to pay for the wood. In most cases people who advertise a "free stuff" ad don't expect you to pay for what you take, but under these stressful circumstances which they are going through I think that offering a symbolic token of appreciation for their generosity is the right thing to do.

The author takes advantage of a "free stuff" pile outside the Masonic Temple of Harlem, N.Y.C.

"Curb alert!"

Curb alert is a phrase used by Craigslist posters to inform fellow Dumpster divers about a pile of furniture, house belongings, sometimes even tools, up for grabs on the street. Because they appear as the subject line on Craigslist ads, just search for "curb alerts" on your local Craigslist site or even request email notifications. Items under curb alert are usually outside someone's house, close to the sidewalk or at the end of the driveway. They're often the leftovers of a garage sale, fall or spring cleanings, or remainders from moving. Curb alerts are free and easy "shopping" opportunities for furniture compo-

nents to incorporate into new pieces, or even for scrap wood.

Of course, what you'll find at the curb alert will vary. It really depends on the circumstances and the care that the person who placed the item on the street had paid. A "Free Stuff" sign may or may not be present, stuff might be arranged nicely in boxes, and furniture may be organized so passersby can easily see their potential. Some people get creative and post signs saying "Take me home," "I'm free and can be yours," and "There's no shame in adopting me." Such thoughtful displays usually lose their "staged" quality after a few pedestrians have sorted through the pile. When

WRAPPING UP

Recently, after responding to a Craigslist ad for free wood scraps, I had the heartfelt experience of meeting a 94-year-old woodworker during a life-changing event: A health crisis preventing him from continuing his passion for the craft. It also left him too feeble to care for his ailing wife of 70 years and the house they lived in for 47 years.

His son Kevin and daughter Kim were in the process of packing up their parents belonging to move them to a small room in the daughter's home in Virginia.

When I arrived at the house, the siblings were working intently on organizing the garage, deciding what was valuable enough to give away and what was trash. I noticed a lot of scrap wood as well as sheets of glass, finishing supplies, old woodworking machines, a portable crane, two workbenches – all the hallmarks of a nice shop. Upon learning that I was a woodworker, Kim pointed out one of the pieces her father built that she was taking back to Virginia. Inside the house she showed me a mid-century reading stand made from walnut. Then she said, "You have to meet my dad!" I waited for him to slowly, but resolutely, descend the few stairs from his bedroom. He was a tall, frail man with long white hair and a beard. Although short of breath he was happy to meet the person who would hopefully make good use of some of his remaining lumber.

He had Kim show me a musical instrument he had built decades ago – a well-built clavichord promised to his other daughter. On the way back to the garage, Kim pointed out dozens of photographs her dad had taken and meticulously framed over the years. I was saddened that this truly talented artist was no longer able to pursue his work.

Back in the garage I sorted through a pile of miscellaneous wood scraps and fished out some nice mahogany, walnut and white oak boards of different shapes and forms. I stayed with the siblings a while longer to lend an ear and offer advice for selling the machinery and hand tools. After saying goodbye I walked back to my car realizing that one day my own family would endure similar circumstances. One spends a life raising a family, tending a garden, building a shop and pursuing a craft and then comes the inescapable decline.

It was an emotional visit and as I drove home my mood was quite somber. But then I realized the gift of witnessing a close and loving family who thoughtfully helped their parents navigate a painful transition. Kim told me that she intended to place her dad's binoculars, a few birdwatching books and some tools in his new room at her home. Who knows, maybe he'll even be able to work on some small-scale projects during the twilight of his life.

A "curb alert" like this can pop up on Craigslist at just about any time. The author spotted this one while driving, and quickly posted the alert himself.

you visit a curb alert, be respectful of the items and to the person who took the time to organize them in the first place. After looking through them, take a few moments to place the stuff you don't want back where you found them as a courtesy to the next person.

I often take pictures of piles that I identify as curb-alert worthy and post them on Craigslist and Facebook to inform fellow Dumpster divers. I encourage you to do the same. It's a great way to conserve valuable resources and keep them from ending up in the landfill.

Navigating the Craigslist website

The Craigslist website provides helpful tools to make a search both focused and convenient. You can specify search parameters such as how much money you're willing to pay or the distance you're willing to drive. You can even set up daily email alerts. For example, I set up a Craigslist's automatic email dispatch to a limited search for "free wood" within a 10-mile radius of my home.

Craigslist shortcomings

The greatest disadvantage of Craigslist is that you have many competitors, which means that everything listed is time-sensitive. By the time you see the ad, contact the owner (in cases where you reply to a "For sale" or "Free stuff" ad) or, in the case of a curb alert, rush to the scene, the items might have already been picked over by early birds who beat you to it.

The other issue with Craigslist is a bit trickier. Most people who sell and buy stuff on Craigslist are honest folks, but a few might be flaky, complicated to communicate with or even deceitful. Sometimes a "Free Stuff" ad is actually a "For Sale" ad purposely misidentified to lure you to click on it, only to find that they're actually attempting to sell their wood. Other Craigslist sellers delay replying to emails, might not be home when you set a time to meet or may completely misrepresent the items they post. Therefore, I suggest you make efforts to verify the authenticity of the ad and attempt to call and talk to the person. If you feel the circumstances are suspicious, avoid the ad altogether or ask a friend to accompany you when you go to see the goods.

The author found this Federal bed at the Nantucket, Mass., "take it or leave it" shed.

These softwood cages were built to protect imported furniture shipped to New York City from overseas. Wood from pallets, cages and containers is among the most common and easiest to find type of wood that can be reclaimed and put to new use.

Freecycle (www.freecycle.org)

Freecycle is a web-based network of groups whose sole interest is to give and receive free stuff. Their site states: "It's a grassroots and entirely nonprofit movement of people who are giving (and getting) stuff for free in their own towns and neighborhoods. It's all about reuse and keeping good stuff out of landfills."

Local Freecycle groups are moderated by local volunteers. The membership is free and, like Craigslist, provides an infrastructure to search for or post items for free. Much like Craigslist, Freecycle allows you to receive email notifications about new listed stuff.

Unlike Craigslist, however, Freecycle is dedicated solely to the exchange of free goods. The network is limited in the number of members compared to Craigslist and has a leaner layout that prevents sending embedded images in their daily email notifications, so you have to visit the listing to see the item. Nevertheless, Freecycle is a wonderful idea and another avenue for us to give and to find reclaimed wood.

Local "take it or leave it" places — recycling centers

I first discovered "take it or leave it" sheds on the island of Nantucket off the coast of Massachusetts almost 15 years ago. Island residents don't have municipal garbage disposal services, and instead pack their trash and recyclables in the car and drive to a community Dumpster at the middle of the island. There, in the parking lot next to where families sort their trash and recyclables into dedicated bins was a big shed for household items, furniture and electrical equipment for giveaway. You'd also often see leftover wood from someone's project there. What a great way to reduce waste and to share resources that otherwise would end up in the abyss of the landfill!

"Take it or leave it" places unfortunately can mostly be found only in small organized communities whose members are well aware of the devastating environmental footprint our trash leaves behind. But that reality should not discourage people who live in less-informed communities from lobbying and encouraging their local government to support such initiatives.

Heavy, solid-wood tables are among the typical fare of free items regularly given away at the Harvard Recycling and Surplus Center at Harvard University.

While the average person might see only scraps for the fireplace in this bin, a woodworker sees a trunk filled with found treasure.

Giveaways by institutions, organizations and towns

For about eight years I served as a Nonresident Tutor of Woodworking and Design at Eliot House at Harvard University in Cambridge, Mass. Eliot House, led at that time by Professor Lino Pertile, is one of 12 undergraduate residential houses on the Harvard campus, and the only house with a functioning woodshop. Our small woodworking program was geared toward Harvard students and affiliates interested in woodworking and furniture design. As the head of the program I was given a small budget that allowed us to keep our volunteer-based shop in order, to buy essential tools and to purchase supplies. To maximize our resources for tools and woodworking machinery I tried to locate as much free wood, shop furniture and supplies as I could get my hands on. Enter the Harvard Recycling and Surplus Center (HRSC).

The HRSC is one of the greatest environmental initiatives that Harvard University has created. It is a warehouse for unwanted lab and office equipment, supplies and materials. Rather than trash these items, Harvard offers them free to the public.

Needless to say that during the years I was affiliated with Harvard and lived in Cambridge, I found many treasures at the HRSC, which we began to refer to affectionately as "The Pound." The HRSC is an example of remarkable vision to better our communities, save our resources and create a positive bond between institutions and the residents of the cities that host them. The more initiatives like this, the better.

Every scrap matters

Scraps are among the most useful building blocks for the reclaimed wood enthusiast. They can be compiled together to make a new canvas for your projects, shaped to make components for a new piece, or used for unique miniature pieces.

When it comes to woodworking scraps, one person's waste is another person's treasure. I've been using scraps from the day I fell in love with woodworking. My first scraps came from the trash of the woodshop where I worked the summer before studying architecture. The shop owner was a family friend who agreed to hire me for four months because of my interest in woodworking and design. Needless to say that as a

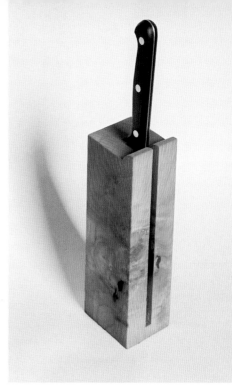

In his woodshop near Jerusalem, Israel, Gil Arad arranges scrap like an architect might lay out buildings in a busy metropolis. This system allows him to identify the pieces' future use according to their length, width and wood species.

Among the author's first efforts using scrap wood is this simple holder for a chef's knife.

temporary employee for such a short stint I hardly had much of a chance to learn the trade. I was told to stay away from the table saw, the jointer and the planer – my job was to carry the tool bags, to sand, to haul lumber and to do practically everything that nobody else wanted to do. While I can't say the experience taught me to be woodworker, I can say it kindled my love of collecting scraps.

The shop I worked in was one of the best in the Tel Aviv area, and architects and interior designers trusted it to provide them with high-end cabinetry and interior work. We worked with solid woods such as oak, ash, mahogany, zebrawood and wenge and I managed to pick up offcuts of varying sizes and shapes. The summer ended and I moved to Haifa and began my study at the Israel Institute of technology.

Toward the end of my five-year degree I gravitated back to woodworking and thought about projects I might build from those scraps. I made a meat-tenderizing mallet for a food aficionado friend, a couple of knife stands, a credit card holder and several other items. After years of working with scraps I still love the challenge of working from small building blocks – of finding and defining purpose for them, or combining them into a tapestry out of which a new and bigger piece will be born.

Reclaimed wood I won't bother with

It may seem by now that I wouldn't hesitate to pick up any available piece of wood or reusable material, but that's not quite the case. For example, furniture made from MDF, chipboard or particleboard, or pieces covered with Formica or melamine are not my cup of tea. In my mind they lack personality, longevity and integrity, and have a limited potential on the reclaimer's pallet.

Further, when many of these manmade industrial wood products are exposed to rain and snow they soak up water like a sponge, then quickly begin to swell and decompose. Real wood that is exposed to water will begin to deteriorate after much longer time, and some species of wood such as white oak, mahogany, teak and black locust are practically rot-resistant.

Chairs wait outside Tom's shop for their turn to become part of the music.

MAKER'S STORIES
Tom Shields' Musical Chairs

Tom Shields of Penland, N.C., is a master of recomposing reclaimed chairs and other found furniture by grouping them into duos, trios, quartets, ensembles and sometimes full orchestras that are harmonious and full of motion, energy and life. Like a genius conductor he is able to let the chairs, which he finds on the side of the road, participate in a sophisticated, often humorous, musical-chairs production that he handcrafts with skill and care.

Like a composer who is attentive to the potential of each individual instrument, Tom knows what each of his chairs can bring to the new composition. With great precision he then ties them together. Sometimes, he needs to add a new part here or there to strengthen their message and uplift even further the furniture/sculptural melody that only he can create.

Tom Shields works on his piece "Off Kilter."

▲ "ONUS" BY TOM SHIELDS (2009)
Found chairs, 140" x 46" x 27"
PHOTOGRAPH BY EDEN REINER

"SECURE" BY TOM SHIELDS (2014) ▶
Found furniture, 30" x 42" x 20"
PHOTOGRAPH BY MERCEDES JELINEK

"OFF KILTER" BY TOM SHIELDS (2012)
Found chairs, 48" x 49" x 39"
PHOTOGRAPH BY STEVE MANN

Kurt Eichhorn's Boat Furniture

Colorful boats like these are a mainstay for fishermen throughout the Indonesian islands.

An All From Boats employee works on salvaging useful wood from a retired boat.

Kurt Eichhorn is a German designer/builder who lives and works on the island of Bali, Indonesia. His company, All From Boats, specializes in repurposing old fishing boats into colorful furniture, and his lively pieces transcend their maritime heritage and bring it ashore and into homes, hotels and commercial spaces.

Eichhorn's furniture is handcrafted from traditional wooden fishing boats that are no longer seaworthy, coffee-tree wood from unproductive recycled coffee trees, and reclaimed iron from old unusable iron drums. In his manifesto he writes, "We do not chop down forests, distress the new wood and call it recycled. And, we never encourage anyone to do so. With our boat wood and coffee tree wood furniture, everyone wins, from the fishermen, to the environment, and to you our clients." Eichhorn firmly believes that his boat-wood furniture has an affirmative effect on countering the rate our planet's resources are consumed, and a positive effect on the communities from which these materials are sourced.

Putting the finishing touches on a small six-drawer chest. Note that much of the boat's appearance – including original paint and even barnacles – remains intact in the finished piece.

Not all of Eichhorn's offerings are large furniture pieces, and may include small items like these colorful hinged boxes.

A six-drawer combination chest and bookcase made by All From Boats.

Through a network of local employees and with a reputation of fairness and consideration, he is able to find and purchase no-longer-seaworthy fishing boats. Built by master Indonesian craftsmen, using time-honored traditional building techniques and locally sourced materials, these boats were once beautiful and important tools for providing the fishermen's families with the resources they need to survive.

But when aging boats become too weak to survive the punishing seas and exhausting schedules, fishermen all over the Indonesian archipelago turn to Eichhorn for help. He is able to purchase their old boats and get these fishermen and their families on their way to building a new boat or starting a different chapter in their lives. The practice is eco-friendly and fair trade.

Indonesia is home for many species of tropical trees that vary in their growth consistency along the coasts and in the inland of this vast islands nation. Therefore boat designs and their woods change from one region to the other but can come from any of the islands of Indonesia, including Bali, Sumatra, Lombok and others.

The boat wood used in All From Boats' furniture ranges from high-grade teak, mahogany, ironwood, and several species that may not be that familiar to American or European woodworkers, such as Assam teak, suar wood or Samanea saman, and mango. His reclaimed boat wood company offers a full line of boat wood furniture, boat wood decorative art, boat wood art, paintings, and even lamps.

CHAPTER 4

Processing Reclaimed Wood
A do-it-yourself guide

With all its charm, rarity and beauty, reclaimed wood can also present several problems and challenges: Embedded metal hardware, high moisture content, contamination by dirt and oils, layers of finish on its surface, and insect infestation make initial cleanup an important part of using this material.

In this chapter I'll talk about the necessary steps needed to turn reclaimed wood into a material you can put to use. I will also discuss creative ways to harness reclaimed wood's unique qualities in your projects.

Your first step in processing reclaimed material is to give it a thorough cleaning to clear away any sand, debris and organic material. Use a vacuum cleaner, a stiff brush, metal picks and hooks, and if necessary clean with water, compressed air or even a pressure washer. After the wood's surface has been thoroughly cleaned you'll likely need to extract old fasteners embedded in it.

Embedded metal hardware
Screws, nails, staples and other metal contaminants are often found in reclaimed material. If the material was originally a structural element in a building, expect it to harbor big nails, screws, hinges and bolts that have most likely corroded over the years. These can be tricky to extract. Some of these blend in with the existing patina so much, or are buried so deeply, that you'll need a metal detector to find them. Nevertheless, it is very important to extract all metal from the wood before milling or resawing. Nails, screws and staples will not only damage

Some embedded metal is visible, but a good handheld metal detector will find things hidden beneath the surface.

◀ Removing soil and fine wood dust from a sill beam that became the author's sculpture "P:91" (presented at the end of this chapter). Most of this dust was actually created as insects bored in and digested the wood. The author used brushes, compressed air and a strong vacuum to clean the delicate and beautiful texture those bugs worked so hard to sculpt.

A thin piece of plywood prevents marring the workpiece.

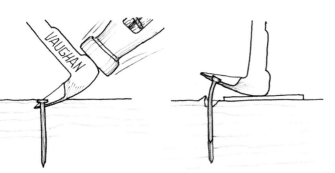

Using a cat's paw.

At left is a typical commercial extractor, at right a pair of narrow-diameter hole saws.

your tools, but present a danger if hit with power equipment.

Nails

If you can easily access the nail heads with a cat's paw, nail puller, claw hammer or pliers, try to extract them slowly and avoid decapitating the heads. When excavating a sunken nail, a cat's paw is more effective than a claw hammer or pliers. If the nail head is below the surface of the wood, push the cat's paw under the head and then leverage it up. Cat's paws of more modern design and those built in the Japanese style have an integral shoulder behind the grabbing claws that

allows you to force the tool under the nail with the help of one or two hammer blows.

A consistent leverage applied by the longest extraction tool whose claws you can place under the nail head is your best strategy. A long tool with a large-swing radius, which is less likely to shear or break the fastener, allows you to apply more power and is easier on your body. It's a common practice to begin extraction with a cat's paw and once the nail has popped up enough, switch to a longer pry bar or a conventional nail puller with a flat sole.

It is always a prudent approach to place a thin piece of

USING A HOLE SAW AS AN EXTRACTOR

Screw extractors such as the ones sold in woodworking catalogs are limited in diameter to no wider than ⅜", so what to do when you have a really wide nail (or screw)? In these cases I use a ⅝" or wider hole-saw. To use a hole-saw successfully, first make a complimentary portable template drilled at the same diameter as the hole-saw exterior.

1 | Remove the center drill bit from the hole saw, and mount the saw in a hand drill.

2 | Center the template's hole over the stubborn fastener, insert the hole saw into the template and drill around the nail.

3 | Set the template aside and continue drilling until you've established a deep enough trench around the nail.

4 | Withdraw and extract the plug. In some cases the fastener is anchored so deep that it refuses to let go. If that's the case, use a small Cat's paw, screwdriver or equivalent tool to break away the wood plug around the nail.

5 | With the nail now exposed and easy to grab, use the tool of your choice to pull it out.

plywood between the extractor and the surface of the wood to prevent the tool from bruising the lumber while you leverage the nail. As the extraction progresses you may need to switch to a thicker piece of wood for your pad to get better leverage.

Some woods, especially oak, have a tendency to hold fasteners so tightly that it feels as if they were fused to the lumber. Corroded nails in oak are probably the toughest to uproot.

If you've exhausted all efforts to extract the nail with a cat's paw, or if there are nails with missing heads, or you broke a head yourself (it will happen, believe me), you may have to resort to removing the stubborn nail along with some of the surrounding wood.

There are some commercially made screw extractors that can help with disobedient nails and screws. The tool looks like a cylinder with rims formed like a saw's teeth. You mount it on a drill and bore a deep circular trench around the nail

Professional reclaimers extract metal fasteners by the thousands.

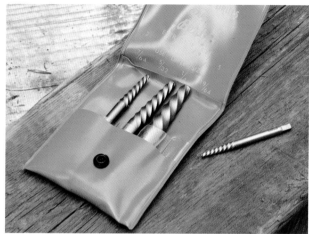

A typical set of screw extractors.

Plunge the spiral cone of an extractor into the screw head and extract the fastener with a counterclockwise twist.

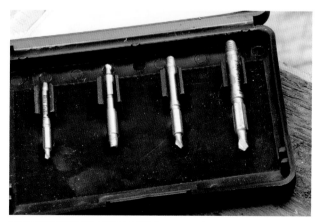

Some extractors have a reverse drill bit on one end.

to isolate it, making it easier to pull out. You can also use a small-diameter hole saw.

Screws and bolts

Bolts and screws cannot be pulled straight out; their threads grab the wood and any attempt to leverage them up will culminate in severe damage to the wood around it, and possibly breakage of the fastener itself. The only way to extract an uncooperative screw or bolt short of removing it along with a chunk of the wood is to unscrew it. Sometimes the head of the bolt or the screw is corroded, deformed or both, making it difficult to grab with a screwdriver or pliers. In these cases you'll need a special extracting tool that grabs the fastener better and allows you to turn it.

A typical extractor looks like a helical cone and works like this: First drill a shallow hole into the head of the fastener; I use a center punch followed by a drill bit. Adding a tiny drop of oil makes drilling easier. Then, using a counterclockwise turn, twist in the specialized extractor. As the spiral cone threads itself into the hole, it bites against the hole's wall and grabs the fastener. As you keep turning counterclockwise it eventually starts turning the fastener counterclockwise, releasing its hold.

No matter what condition a pallet is in, you can count on there being dozens of nails in each.

Nail pullers comes in all sizes and shapes. Some of the new designs excel at specific tasks, such as the Crescent Bull Bar. A wide-clawed, long handled tool like this makes dismantling pallet wood and deck boards much easier.

Some of these tools are extractors only, while others are a combination with a short counterclockwise drill bit on one end and the spiral extraction cone on the other.

Processing quality pallet wood

Pallet reclaims are easy to get and usually cost nothing. If you follow a local Craigslist or Freecycle group you'll see a few posted every week for free. Most of these pallets are within the standard sizes of 36" x 36", or 40" x 48". The lumber used in pallets is mostly a cocktail of softwood and low-grade hardwood. However, occasionally you might get your hands on irregular-sized pallets or pallets made from better wood. In general, I don't make use of common wood pallets but when I see a high-end pallet around – and especially a pallet composed of thick runners (the carrying beams) and straight-grain boards – I take the time to dismantle it and save the wood.

Pallet lumber is often nailed with all manner of twisted nails that make the extraction difficult. You'll have to use long-handled tools and pry bars, or buy a dedicated pallet and deck-board extractor such as the one pictured. If you don't have one of these specialized tools you still can try to extract the nails using a cat's paw, hammer and pry bar or even saw them free from the runners.

A mallet helps loosen nails.

A technique that helps me pop up the nails without resorting to a cat's paw is thumping the boards from the back using a non-marring mallet. I begin by pounding the boards from their underside, nudging and pushing them out a half an inch or so. This makes it easier to slip a pry-bar's claw underneath before emancipating them. If I feel a board might crack or

Dan Marsch of Shady, N.Y., air-dries his lumber on elevated racks underneath his barn. By allowing natural airflow between the boards and slabs for a year or two the moisture content of the lumber gradually drops to 15% or 20%, suitable for most construction projects.

A pair of typical moisture meters.

break I tap it back flush with the surface of the runner in hope that the nail's head remains proud of the surface for easier extraction. Once the nail's head reveals itself, grab it with a claw hammer or a pry-bar and pull it out.

Moisture and reclaimed lumber

Throughout history lumber for furniture and carpentry has been dried in the open air, in sheds and under roofed structures. This brought the lumber moisture content to around 15% to 20%, which was, and still is, sufficient for a good deal of work. Before the invention of wood-drying kilns, a woodworker wanting to reduce the moisture content of lumber even further to make it more stable needed to bring the lumber indoors for an additional period of drying. You can still do it that way, but a kiln greatly expedites drying. With the help of a kiln – either a commercial one or one you build – you could reduce the moisture content of freshly cut timber, reclaimed lumber and wood that has been exposed to moisture to around 8% which is suitable for most woodworking projects.

How dry does reclaimed wood need to be?

Wood bought at the lumberyard for making furniture,

flooring and interior projects must be dry enough for the modern home setting. Most homes in the developed world have heating and air conditioning systems that keep the air relatively dry. If we build woodworking projects for the home environment with lumber that's not dry enough, we risk unintended structural and joint deformations that will afflict the project as the wood shrinks while subjected to the dry interior conditions. This can even lead to jeopardizing the structural integrity of the project. Therefore, for most furniture and interior projects we need to reduce the moisture content of reclaimed wood to around 8%. There are exceptions to this rule, such as when building Windsor chairs. The makers of these chairs actually prefer to work with air-dried wood for the seat and other components. After construction the chair continues to dry and shrink around the legs and all the interconnected parts, increasing structural strength.

Other indoor projects that can be made with wood of higher moisture content include sculptural work, bowls, bentwood elements, and massive-timber and live-edge furniture where the future deformation – resulting from drying, shrinkage and checks – naturally becomes part of their charm.

Moisture content in reclaimed wood

Pallet wood, timber used in barns and roofs or the outdoors, as well as lumber that was exposed to rain or snow will probably have a moisture content around 15% or higher. That means that you can work with this wood to build rustic and outdoor projects, or any project whose future shrinkage due to continual reduction of moisture content will not be detrimental to its integrity or design.

But if I were to use wooden pallets and other thin timber for building indoor furniture, I'd let the boards acclimate in a dry environment for a few months, allowing the moisture to drop before milling and working it into the new piece. This allows the lumber to shrink and settle. To help reduce reclaimed wood moisture content fast and efficiently, place it in a room or in an enclosed space with a dehumidifier. As the dehumidifier absorbs moisture from the air, water from the lumber migrates out and is condensed by the dehumidifier.

I keep some of my reclaimed lumber in a crawl space under our house along with a dehumidifier. The dehumidifier not only keeps the moisture down to prevent mold growth, but also is instrumental in reducing the moisture content of my reclaimed wood.

If I'm working with wood that has been exposed heavily to rain, and whose moisture content exceeds 15% I let the lumber acclimate for a year more, depending on its thickness. It is also possible to resaw the reclaimed wood on a bandsaw to create thinner boards that acclimate more quickly.

If you're creating small parts, turned elements and the like, you might be able to fit the moist wood into a microwave. A few cycles of heating the piece, letting it cool and heating it again will allow water to migrate. This can take from one to five days, depending on the thickness of the blank.

In a recent reclaimed coffee table project, I needed to turn a walnut leg from a reclaimed beam that had stood in the rain for a long time. To make the drying process more efficient I turned the blank to the rough dimensions of the intended leg design and then began the heating/drying intervals in the microwave. I microwaved the leg for three to five minutes on a medium setting, then let it cool down for a few hours before repeating. Once the measurable moisture content had dropped to 8%-10% I brought the leg back to the lathe and

Metering moisture on a recent pallet acquisition shows a moisture content of 16% — not surprising for a wooden item left outdoors.

Microwaving, when done carefully, speeds up the drying process for rough turnings. Once the moisture content reaches the desired level, it's back to the lathe to complete the turning.

turned it to its final shape.

By roughly shaping the object before putting it into the microwave, I was able to save a lot of energy and time during the process of drying the leg. This technique of rough shaping, then a drying period followed by final shaping is very common among woodturners who make bowls from greenwood. Greenwood moisture content is very high. The turner roughly shapes the bowl, then dries it either by placing it in paper bags or dry wood chips, or by using the microwave technique. As the bowl dries it deforms – a perfectly round bowl will become oval.

PLUG CUTTING BASICS

1 | Mount a plug cutter in your drill or drill press to make some plugs.

2 | Use a screwdriver or other implement to snap the plug out of the wood.

3 | Drilling the matching hole in the workpiece should be done either on the drill press or using a stable template, preferably clamped to the workpiece to prevent the drill from wandering. This is especially important when you enlarge an existing hole in the workpiece. For example, let's assume you used an extractor to release a stubborn screw from the lumber. During the process you created a $3/8$" hole you want plugged, but you only have $1/2$" plugs so

you have to enlarge the hole with a $1/2$" drill bit. The best drill bit for the job is a Forstner bit, but a Forstner bit isn't easy to center in the void of the $3/8$" hole. To make the task easier, drill a template with a $1/2$" hole, then center the template over the $3/8$" hole and drill through.

4 | Then apply glue on the plug and on the rims of the hole, orient the plug with the grain of the surrounding wood and tap it in.

5 | Once the glue has dried you can saw off the excess plug stock.

6 | When dry, plane, sand or scrape the surface smooth.

After verifying with a moisture meter that the bowl has reached the 8%-10% moisture content, the turner mounts it again on the lathe to bring it to its final shape.

Plugging holes and sealing cracks

In some reclaimed wood projects one doesn't need to plug screws or nails holes if the rough, authentic surface is part of the intended design. Showing patinated boards that are gray and distressed, boards with traces of paint on them, contaminated with oils or writing can be an integral part of a bold artistic statement. But in many other instances you may want to plug the holes to create an uninterrupted and harmonious

grain flow on the surface of your project.

Contrary to what may seem natural to do, you should wait until you finish milling the reclaimed lumber to your project specifications before plugging any holes. If you plug the raw lumber immediately after extracting the fasteners you run the risk of needing to replug it later after jointing and planing the wood. During the milling process you could end up shaving too much of the plug and it may lose its purchase on the wood.

To plug successfully you need a well-made plug and an accurately drilled hole to accept it. You can buy plug cutters in a variety of widths, but you can also turn a plug on the lathe. If your intent is to have the plug blend in with the grain

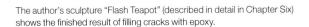

The author's sculpture "Flash Teapot" (described in detail in Chapter Six) shows the finished result of filling cracks with epoxy.

A bit of wax at the end of the crack keeps thin epoxy from oozing out.

Leveling an epoxy fill.

and color of the wood, make sure to choose the wood you make your plug from carefully. If you keep an offcut from the original reclaimed lumber you were working with, you can use it as your plug block.

Dealing with cracks and voids

You can secure thin cracks by gently prying them open and filling them with super glue, wood glue or epoxy. The glue or epoxy will flow into minor cracks with gravity and capillary action, and with the help of a clamp to close the seam line tight they'll virtually disappear.

But when dealing with broader cracks a better solution is a filler of wood glue mixed with fine sawdust like the kind found in sander dust bags. A thin-blade artist's spatula works well for persuading these thicker substances into cracks. For big cracks, missing wood, empty knotholes and the like, I've had good results with an epoxy resin. I like to add color pigment to the epoxy, but using clear epoxy or epoxy tinted with wood colorant is another option. The pigment adds interest to the repair by rendering it a design feature and turning it into a focal point, rather than trying to hide the defect by coloring the epoxy with wood dyes. My epoxy of choice is a thin, slow-setting formula that allows the mixed fluid to penetrate into the deepest crevices.

Before filling the crack with epoxy, thoroughly clean it out. Pick out large pieces with an awl or other sharp tool, then us a high-speed rotary tool such as a Dremel to clear away any loose wood fibers or contaminants.

When filling with epoxy, it's important to seal the ends and undersides of any crack or hole to keep the epoxy from seeping out. My first choice is plain masking tape, but if the area is too rough for the tape to adhere, shipping tape pressed over by a rubber pad and a clamp works well. For small end grain cracks I might dab in a bit of paste wax. The blob of wax hardens and prevents the epoxy from dripping out.

While hewing this beam, the author exposed a colony of carpenter ants.

This tiny powder post beetle easily fits on the point of a standard pencil. Note the holes the beetles created in the wood.

Picture of a spalted tabletop which was inflicted by powder post beetles.

When the epoxy has nearly hardened slice off high spots with a sharp chisel. Once fully cured, sand the surface smooth. In many cases I seal the cracks during the initial stages of surfacing the reclaimed wood and let the jointer and planer shave away the epoxy until it's level with the surface.

Insects

Insects, while important to our ecosystem, can be quite a nuisance if they decide to make a home inside your home. Reclaimed wood can be a habitat for a few types of wood burrowers including termites, carpenter ants, bark and cambium munchers, and powder post beetles. Let's discuss how to deal with these six-legged invaders.

Termites

Termite-infested reclaimed wood is mostly a problem for softwood post-and-beam timbers. You'll typically find them in barns and old houses' sill beams placed on or close to the ground. Termites flourish in hierarchical colonies – this means that if during the process of reclaiming the wood the colony was separated from its monarch, the individual termites will perish. In addition, if we dry and heat up the lumber we will most likely eradicate the termites. The same approach works when used for carpenter ants.

Wood-boring beetles

Most beetle varieties have a special liking for sapwood – the new growth of fibrous structural tissue under the bark. It is soft and high in starch and nitrogen, which is essential for the larva's development. However, most wood-boring insects cannot survive in a dry environment, and once the lumber moisture content drops below 12% the beetles' larva find it difficult to digest the fibers and die. There are exceptions, of course; the notorious lyctid powder post beetle's larva can survive in lumber with moisture content as low as 8%.

By and large, keeping the lumber in a dry environment eventually drops the moisture content to a point where the larvae aren't able to survive. If you need the lumber for immediate use you can quickly eradicate insects by kiln drying or exposing it to a heat source.

Other methods of heating wood include placing it in a dark box outside in the sun for a few hours on a hot summer day, steaming it in a steam box or microwaving it on a short but high heating cycle.

Finished reclaimed wood

Many kinds of reclaimed wood such as floorboards, found furniture, house siding, and painted posts and beams are covered with layers of finish. This finish can be old or new, transparent or opaque, strongly adhered to the original wood or loose and flaky.

If your project will celebrate the old patina and finish of

Designer Erica Diskin made this restaurant hostess stand from old door panels, leaving the original paint intact.

USING A CHEMICAL STRIPPER

1 | Apply stripper.

2 | Spread stripper over wood surface.

3 | Allow to work for time specified in container directions.

4 | Repeat as needed.

reclaimed wood, you should not remove it. However, if the paint is flaky and loose you should consider stabilizing it by spraying or brushing on a sealer coat of some kind – matte varnish works well. You can also carefully sand the surface without removing too much of the authentic finish before applying a new layer of protective clear finish of your choice.

Complete removal of old finish

If the finish is opaque and old, there may be layers of paint that include lead. If possible, skin the paint away by resawing the reclaimed wood just enough to get rid of the layers of paint and a minimum amount of wood underneath. I would not advise sanding the finish or removing it with a heat gun but if you must do it to preserve as much of the original wood as possible, take the appropriate personal and environmental

safety measures. Use up-to-code safety equipment, such as respirators and dust masks to avoid breathing paint dust, connect your sander to a dust collector, and protect your skin from the harmful dust.

Another approach to removing old paint is to strip it chemically with a paint stripper. There are a few types of chemical strippers comprising different formulas. In general the slower, less-potent strippers are the safest. I prefer to use the more modern and environmentally friendly strippers such as 3M Safest Striper when I work indoors, and a fast-acting stripper when I work outside. Most modern strippers have a jelly-like consistency that allows them to sit on both horizontal and moderately tilted surfaces. I prefer to use a stripper that can be cleaned with water after it has been scraped off, making it easier to clean the wood.

Resawing reclaimed wood in layers reveals a distinct look with each layer.

Read the instructions carefully before using any stripper and comply with all environmental and personal safety precautions. You need to protect your skin, lungs and eyes, as paint stripper can be harmful. The 3M and other water-based strippers will evaporate if left on the surface for a prolonged period of time or under the sun. This is why I keep a spray bottle filled with water and spritz the surface as needed to keep the stripper active. It might take one or two stripping cycles to completely remove the layers of paint that have been applied to the wood over the years.

You can also use a heat gun to strip away old finishes. Direct the hot air onto the surface and use a scraper or putty knife to scrape away the paint as the heat softens it.

Transparent coatings

If your reclaimed wood is sealed with a transparent coat of oil-based finish, shellac, lacquer, varnish, epoxy or polyester, you can try the following techniques to strip it:

- Skin the finish with a bandsaw
- Strip it with a paint striper or with a heat gun
- Sand it away
- Use a dedicated solvent (in the case of shellac or lacquer)

Shellac

Shellac is one of the oldest wood finishes and is applied mainly on furniture. Shellac's solvent of choice is denatured alcohol. By rubbing the surface with steel wool or synthetic abrasive pad dampened with alcohol, you'll gradually dissolve the shellac as well as any wax that was applied. Scrub the surface with the pad and absorb the thick, sticky shellac-alcohol "mud." When the finish no longer reacts to the alcohol you've probably reached the bare wood. Now, wet a rag with alcohol and give the wood a final wiping down. For safety, be sure to wear appropriate gloves and have adequate ventilation to prevent the alcohol fumes from lingering.

Lacquer

Lacquer is used mainly for finishing furniture. Like shellac, lacquer is an evaporative finish. It is dissolved using acetone or paint thinner. The stripping process is much like the one used for shellac. For safety, use gloves and work in open air or provide adequate ventilation to prevent the acetone fumes from lingering – acetone fumes are highly volatile and toxic.

Oil-based finishes/varnish

Oil-based finishes and varnishes may be used to finish wooden floorboards, furniture, wooden paneling in walls and ceilings. Linseed oil, varnishes and a combination of the two can be sanded off or removed with a heat gun or a paint striper. Follow the same methods you would for stripping opaque finishes.

Polyester/Epoxy

Polyester and epoxy finishes are the toughest of finishes and are a headache to remove. Some paint strippers may not affect them at all so you will have to use a heat gun, or just sand them away. Use the strictest of safety measures when dealing with these finishes.

Resawing Thick Reclaimed Lumber

When exposed to the elements for years or even decades, some species of wood present deep checks and a rough, dark surface. These weathered planks provide the avid reclaimer with at least four types of unique subcategories of reclaimed surfaces:

PAINT WITH A PAST

A popular technique of festively incorporating painted Heritage Reclaimed wood is to sand randomly through the many layers of paint that have covered the piece over the years. This exposes the archaeological legacy of the object and allows us to see the different colors and finishing materials previous owners have applied. It denotes its history and tells a thing or two about fashion, taste and use.

Gilad Erjaz, a prolific reclaimed-wood cabinetmaker in Israel, enhances many of his projects by incorporating Heritage Reclaimed wood still covered by many layers of paint. One of Gilad's techniques to is to randomly unveil the layers one by one, allowing areas of paint and wood to coexist. The outcome, such as the entrance doors to a newly built restaurant, is striking with the exposed vintage paint taking on a '"Damascus" appearance. Gilad uses this technique on projects such as wall coverings, panel doors, drawer fronts and boxes.

Careful sanding of years-old paint left these doors far more interesting that the original paint job likely did.

- **Unprocessed, aged reclaimed wood surface, rustic and rough** – the raw outer layer of the reclaimed wood
- **Skimmed reclaimed** – shaving off a thin layer (in essence the proud ridges and peaks) from the aged surface using a planer or a sanding belt yields a flatter surface with smooth, lighter color on top and darker, rougher patina on the lower areas.
- **Checked core** – resawing the lumber to a depth where checks are still present creates a unique look where the checks' remains slither randomly throughout the board's face
- **Core** – resawing the lumber deeper below the checked layer affords you a good chance of exposing the pristine core wood

As an example of this technique, take a look at the photo on the previous page. Gilad Erjaz purchased reclaimed flatbed timber that was once flooring for Austrian freight cars. By resawing the white oak beams as described above he managed to create a variety of distinct reclaimed looks from rustic and rough, to pristine and virgin.

Ply-reclaimed: Reclaimed wood as Veneer

We can maximize the potential of reclaimed wood by resaw-

Woodworker Gilad Erjaz created the unique look for the surface of these boards by gluing thin slices of reclaimed lumber atop ordinary plywood.

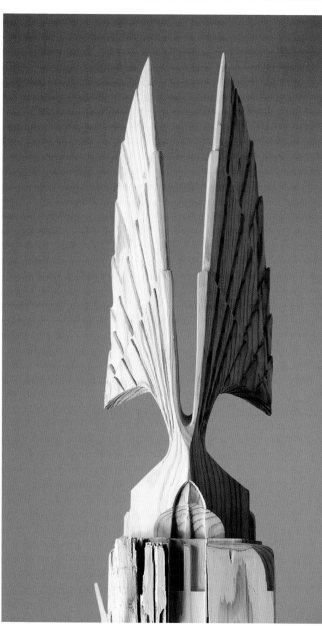

"P:91" BY YOAV LIBERMAN (2011)
Reclaimed pine beam, reclaimed aromatic cedar, found bronze mail box
door, reclaimed Mediterranean cypress, reclaimed concrete crag
11" x 16" x 91"
PHOTOGRAPH BY BILL HOO

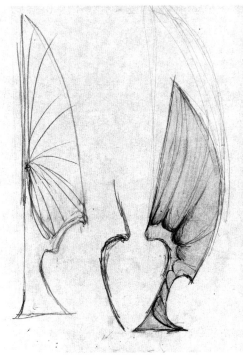

This piece is about that fundamental human yearning for good tidings and the resurrection of form and matter from decomposition into the sublime.

After saving a discarded sill beam removed during the renovation of an old farmhouse and examining it closely, I concluded that being close to the ground and surrounded by moisture, the beam became heavily infested by termites or carpenter ants. The insects favored the lush and soft early-wood, leaving behind the harder and thinner latewood that grew over the summers.

The outcome was a fragile feathery terrain that transformed this construction-grade beam into an intriguing work of art even without my intervention. But it also provided me with an opportunity to turn it into a tall totem-like sculpture, informed by Art Deco architecture and, in particular, the shape of the Empire State Building in New York City.

The heroic Art Deco era is filled with towering achieve-ments: bigger than life structures, lofty and luminescent – an array of "streamlined" designs that are reductive, yet figurative. The Empire State Building's designers envisioned a mooring tower that allowed passengers to embark and disembark from a hovering airship. The tower's massive wings acted as buttresses, built to provide structural and aesthetic support to it. The form of these wings was both symbolic and practical, as fit the iconic design that proliferated in the early – and exciting – days of aviation.

Had it actually been used as a docking port, the architects and engineers might have been credited with constructing not only the most iconic building ever to grace the New York City skyline, but also the most spectacular technological achieve-ment of its time. However, in the end no airships took on or deployed passengers from there.

Nevertheless, the attempt to dream and hope, the aesthet-ics and the symbolic nature of the wings on the spire of, at

The author's friend, wood sculptor Steff Rocknak, shows off the ready-to-work beam.

Using a router jig to cut the beam details and facets.

The author bores a hole in the concrete chunk to mount the beam.

The first step was to thoroughly clean the reclaimed sill beam of all loose insect debris and rotted wood.

the time, the world's highest building, is a truly remarkable achievement. This is even more impressive if we realize that this building was built during the bleak years of the Depression. Yet as we sometimes see, when in dire straights society (and individuals) can excel and ascend. Raising their hopes to the skies, they search for answers and deliverance in the heavens and under the wings of metaphorical angels.

My totem has its footing on a broken slab of concrete, salvaged from a construction site. Close to the ground the sill beam displays an unadulterated organic, feather-like texture, much like on the day that I found it. As it ascends higher and higher it becomes narrower and slimmer, re-formed into a work of architecture that bears smoother surfaces and thoughtful proportions. Then we reach the mailbox.

I found its door on the street near my old apartment in Cambridge, Mass., and built for it a special cedar box that resides in a dedicated cavity at the heart of the totem. The ornamental mailbox is, by itself, an allegory to the funda-

5

The finished beam, ready for the post office box door and the winged topper.

6

The wings, rough-cut on the band saw.

7

Rough-shaping the wings with mallet and chisel.

mental human yearning for deliverance, for a good omen, an important message, or perhaps a letter or email which will change our lives for the better?

Deliverance, Providence, and Salvation – not necessarily in their religious meaning – are fundamental human aspirations. Most of us, when in trouble or in doubt, wish that via the magic of a miracle, by chance, or through sheer luck, things will change for the better. Some pray to a deity, while others put their trust in science, or in reason, or turn to friends and counselors. The mailbox is a collective representation for these aspirations.

As the totem continues to climb we finally reach the wings. Heavily saturated with symbolism, the wings were the most challenging part to design and build. They were carved by my friend Steff Rocknak, a brilliant wood sculptor and philosopher. They crown the totem with an angelic apex, reminding us that people have always aspired to reach to the skies both metaphorically and literally.

8

Steff Rocknak uses a rotary tool to do the detail carving on the wings.

CHAPTER 5

Salvaged/Recovered Wood
Finders, keepers… makers

Salvaged/Recovered wood includes driftwood from river banks or seashores, sunken logs, unexpected fallen trees, dead or dying trees that pose an imminent threat to houses and property, branches that fall to the ground after a storm, and even stacks of "free firewood" by the side of the road. Reclaims of this kind can be used as-is for sculptural objects, art pieces, raw material for bowl turning and, if the salvaged material is big enough, even be resawn or hewn into boards and slabs.

Urban salvation

The fastest growing trend in the reclaimed-wood world is lumber salvaged from urban settings. In many cities in this country and abroad, homeowners and city governments are becoming aware that fallen trees, trees that need to be cut down because of developmental needs, and trees that are dead or diseased and cannot be rehabilitated can still be a valuable resource. In the past, felled urban trees were usually turned into mulch or simply hauled away to the landfill.

But today, with the growing awareness for resource preservation and a demand for using local materials, there is an incentive to reuse urban lumber. Businesses involved in urban salvation might arrive on the site of a fallen tree to limb and cut it into manageable portions. Depending on accessibility and location they might mill logs into slabs on the spot, or haul them to an urban lumberyard for milling and processing. Most urban salvation lumberyards include a kiln where the slabs can be dried, and perhaps a small woodshop where customers can buy wood and have it sawn to their specific design dimensions.

Oded Keets' "Cypresstool" uses reclaimed cypress with minimal processing of the raw material.
ODED KEETS

The lumber produced in an urban mill is unique and irregular. The life story of each urban tree is very particular and the circumstances that brought it to the end of its life are very specific. Because expedience is an important factor in clearing fallen trees from densely populated neighborhoods, the salvaged logs are generally shorter than commercial logs obtained from forests.

Salvaged/Recovered Wood **89**

A dead ash tree between houses in Woodstock, N.Y. This dead tree is yet another casualty to the infamous emerald ash borer that's slowly destroying ash trees in the Northern hemisphere.

"Mulberry Trio" slab and console table. This is a truly organic table that highlights both the contrasts and the harmoniousness of its elements. The top, made from a tree that fell in New York City, provides rustic warmth, while the white legs, made from reformed oak, teak, maple, and mahogany, are classical and austere.

Slabs produced from trees that die of disease may include voids, patches of decay and other irregularities that you don't typically see in commercial lumber. Trees growing near fences eventually swallow them; lumber harvested from such trees may include hidden metal parts that a sawyer must extract before milling them. While these complications may be impediments for the commercial woodworker, artists, makers and woodworkers who work with live-edge lumber may view such irregularities as blessings in disguise.

Salvation reclaims DIY (the Soybel-Bartges homestead)

My friend Dan Marsch spends his summers in Shady, N.Y., a beautiful village in the Catskill Mountains. There, surrounded by forests, meadows and mountains, he works hard to preserve and improve an old homestead that has been in the possession of his partner's family for many decades.

Dan is a Renaissance man – farmer, lumberjack and sawyer. During the summer he works as a carpenter, and is a busy high school math teacher during the rest of the year. He has

The Soybel-Bartges homestead in upstate New York. By milling dead, diseased or recently fallen trees, Dan Marsch is able to build and restore structures, fences and equipment all around the property.

Dan Marsch built this storage shed entirely out of salvaged wood

Dan milling wood on a portable band saw.

◀ The hemlock woolly adelgid disease struck many of the eastern hemlock trees at Dan's homestead and across the East Coast. This tiny insect kills the trees by depriving them of essential sap. Here is a branch showing this silent killer as areas of bluish plume.

▲ Emerald ash borer exit holes on the bark of an ash tree, a sure sign that this tree is on its deathbed. These insect larvae decimate the tree's thin growth tissue and prevent nutrients from reaching the leaves. (Right) Once ash bark is removed you can see the crisscross pattern of the channels that larvae dig throughout their lifespan underneath the bark.

vast knowledge of botany, agricultural history, timber frame building and reclaiming wood from dead or dying trees. The woods surrounding the farm are spotted with diseased or dead hemlock and ash trees that Dan reclaims if they've fallen or are at risk of collapsing. He cuts off the limbs and hauls them with his tractor to his portable bandsaw mill. He skins the logs on four sides, then slices them to make slabs and boards, then stores them underneath his barn and after a year or two the lumber is dry enough for rustic woodworking and carpentry projects.

The author's son, Asher, enjoys an afternoon snack on a pile of reclaimed logs.

Logs placed on pressure treated lumber in the author's backyard. A tarp tensioned on top of the pile with weights (or nailed to the logs by the grommets) helps protect logs from rain and snow.

Salvaged/Recovered from your backyard

Most of my Salvaged/Recovered pieces were saved from our neighborhood and our backyard. I try to keep my eyes open and occasionally I spot firewood logs on the curb after a recent visit by an arborist to a neighbor's yard. There is a limit to what I am able to carry and frankly I don't want to risk my 50-plus-year-old back unnecessarily (I need to save my back and lifting capabilities for my growing toddler son), so I try to pick up only manageable size logs and branches.

A year ago after three of our dead or damaged trees had to come down because they presented a risk to our house, I asked the arborist to chop the massive oak and birch trunks into six- or eight-foot long logs. Then, with the help of a peavey hook I maneuvered the logs over a makeshift sleeper bed that I put on the ground for them to rest upon. I plan on using the logs for making a shaving horse or a bowl-making workbench, chopping platforms, big Scandinavian style

bowls, and other primitive furniture or contraptions. If I invest in a portable mill, and if I can keep these logs unharmed by fungi and insects, they could yield a nice crop of slabs and boards. In the meantime, I try to keep leaves and water away from the logs, so recently I placed a tarp on top of them secured with weights or nails.

Branches can also be used for making all kinds of small woodworking projects such as mallets, spoons, fences and gates for the yard, and some other small-scale projects.

My collection of salvaged logs and branches gave me the opportunity to experiment with green woodworking, which refers to shaping lumber and timber that retains a high level of saturated water and moisture from when the tree was still alive. With an axe or hewing hatchet it is quite possible to shape the log and square it up. If you want to invest in an adze, you'll be able to stand on the logs and comfortably flatten facets on them that will eventually create a beam.

After a neighbor cut down a dead tree, the author placed some of the short logs on branches to prevent them for direct contact with the ground.

"OUT OF THE MOUTHS OF BABES AND SUCKLINGS"

On our way back from daycare I sometimes take my son on the longer route home instead of zipping through a major artery. I prefer the more winding roads with the shady trees above and the occasional deer or turkey that crosses our path. I like to look at the houses and the trees which I point out to my son Asher, identifying them and asking him to repeat their names, which he is happy to do. I tell him how important they are to our world and to our village.

Recently, one of the houses on our route was sold. This house was surrounded by half an acre or so of woodland flourishing with magnificent decades-old trees that provide a nurturing habitat for our wildlife. The new owners stormed in and leveled the woodland, leaving only three or four trees standing. I really could not understand why this had to happen – were the owners planning to build a swimming pool or a tennis court on their lot? But even if they did, surely with the help of a talented landscape architect this destruction could have been avoided or at least scaled down significantly. But, unfortunately, that wasn't the case. So one evening, at the aftermath of the catastrophe when we passed near this house and saw the silent massive root bases, logs, and limbs of oak, maple, beach and birch that littered the ground, I said to Asher, "This is so sad, so sad."

Ever since then whenever we pass by this house I hear him chant those words from the backseat, reminding me of the capricious and often irresponsible way we treat our environment. Let's hope that by the time Asher's generation is behind the steering wheel things will change for the better.

Olive wood log, cleaned and ready for sculpting.

Liran Vanunu uses a grinder to shape an olive wood sofa.

MIRI VINTER

LIRAN VANUNU OLIVE WOOD FURNITURE

Liran Vanunu is an Israeli woodworker based in the Galilee region who specializes in crafting millennia-old olive trees that have died and been salvaged, and turning them into furniture. His tool pallet is made mostly of a chainsaw along with a power grinder and some sanders that he deploys on the aged olive trunks and limbs. The organic lace-like matrix of ancient olive timber is both fascinating and exclusive to this type of tree. But it also presents to the artist some major structural challenges, as the wooden matrix may be too dry, checked and fragile, causing it to break off during the process of shaping it.

Liran starts by thoroughly cleaning the character-saturated logs' exteriors and interiors – including all the tiny inner voids – of accumulated dirt, sand and stones. Then he examines the remaining shape and outlines a course of action to guide his chainsaw. After rough-shaping the furniture he commences with the laborious work of rough sanding, which follows by finish sanding and concludes with a few coats of finish.

Let it spalt, let it spalt, let it spalt

If you want to preserve your Salvaged/Recovered wood inventory, make every effort to protect it from dampness, rain and snow. Elevate it from the ground and prevent leaves, branches and soil from accumulating on it, as insects and rot favor moisture and will move in to munch on your lumber in no time.

Perhaps the only advantage of letting logs and branches lay on the ground for extended periods of time is that once you turn, split or mill them, you may find some beautiful colors and texturing thanks to the infiltration of an artistic fungi.

Fed by moisture from rain, soil and inside the log itself, as well as by sugars in the lumber, the clandestine fungi will work its way into the heart of the wood. On its elusive route, and around it, it transforms the color of the lumber, creating veins of black, clouds of gray, and a variety of other splendid and abstract shapes and patterns. But beware, if you expose the log to water for too long the fungi will eventually spread too much, soften the wood and invite rot. So, try to monitor its progression (or regression, as the case may be) before making use of or milling the lumber, then let it dry before the wood turns into a pale spongy mash.

Civic trees

City trees are the biggest organisms that grow in our civic space. These ever-changing perennial giants nourish our lives and make our parks and streets meaningful and enjoyable. Many of us develop a close relationship with these trees as we get to know them, walk by them or sit under them.

But when the cycle of life dictates that a civic tree is no longer safe to remain standing, an honorable outcome is absolutely possible. Delivered by the skilled hands of "urban reclaimers" these trees can become works of art and craft. When a tree is just too old or ill or damaged by a storm to be viable, a company like Re-Co Bklyn can carefully cut down the tree, resaw it and sell the lumber so the tree can live on for generations in our homes and workspaces.

Roger Benton's and Dan Richfield's mission in life is to save our local trees from the "waste stream," as Dan calls it. Since almost all of the urban trees that Re-Co Bklyn salvages aren't desirable by the lumber industry, without their efforts those trees would have been chopped to pieces for mulch or

The author stored these birch branches outside during the winter. When rived in the summer, spalting fungi had already begun to enchant the wood.

"Penland Table," co-designed by the author and Patrick Kana, displays a marvelous spalting pattern.

Reclaimed trees cut down and sawn into slabs.

Roger Benton and Dan Richfield of Re-Co Bklyn stand in front of reclaimed trees harvested in New York City.

A slab from one of Re-Co Bklyn's salvaged trees was turned into this attractive dining table.

Re-Co-Bklyn harvesting a section of dead elm tree known as "the second largest tree in New York City."

"The second largest tree in New York City" being cut into slabs.

turned into firewood. But with hard work, a healthy appetite for preservation and an artistic vision, they manage to repurpose the trees into beautiful lumber and some great looking pieces of furniture.

In 2015 Roger and Dan met their biggest challenge (so far). Via Andrew Ullman, Brooklyn's Director of Forestry, they were introduced to the second largest tree in the Five Boroughs, a dead European elm that had to be taken down. The circa-1870 tree was intentionally planted in a quiet southwestern corner of Prospect Park in Brooklyn. Two years after the tree was declared dead it was cut down, and at that point they were invited to salvage it with the intent to bestow it with a prosperous future.

Quoting Dan: "This tree is one of the few things in

BLACK COTTON SIDE TABLE

For this live-edge project I created an inverted "U"-shaped side table from a narrow slab of cottonwood that fell during the onslaught of hurricane Sandy on New York City. After Re-Co Bklyn milled and kiln-dried the tree into lumber I visited their yard and noticed an odd-shaped reject slab that was just too narrow for most commercial woodworking applications.

I bought the slab for little money and devised a plan to cut it into three segments connected via waterfall miter joints at the intersections of the top and the legs. To highlight the table's live-edge narrative and to increase the definition of design and shape upon the wood grain I decided to stain the furniture with pitch-black die.

"BLACK COTTON SIDE TABLE" BY YOAV LIBERMAN (2013)
Cottonwood, ebony pigment, shellac, oil, 12" x 34" 32"
PHOTOGRAPH BY YOAV LIBERMAN

The "Black Cotton Side Table" started out as this reject slab the author got for a bargain.

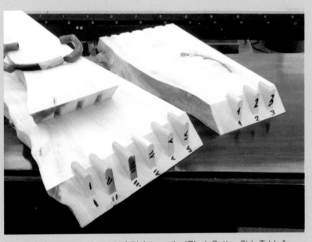

Loose tenons secure the waterfall joints on the "Black Cotton Side Table."

NYC that had remained unchanged for that century and a half. Think about it. When planted, dirt roads, horses and farmland surrounded it. By the end of its life, it neighbored a gas station taking credit card transactions and nearly every person walking around it had a smartphone in their pocket."

In a remarkable closure of a life cycle, slabs from this NYC treasure have been reintroduced to the New York community,

including an impressive conference table that was custom built in gratitude to the N.Y.C. Parks, Prospect Park Offices in Litchfield Villa.

Mitch Ryerson sits in the Lee St. "stump throne," the largest he's made to date.

The Lee St. stump throne has weathered to a soft gray patina over the years.

MAKER'S STORIES
Mitch Ryerson

Mitch Ryerson was my first mentor. He is a prolific studio-furniture maker who creates indoor and outdoor furniture of sculptural quality. In recent years, Mitch has spent most of his energy building whimsical playground contraptions, outdoor benches and artistic chairs from tree stumps.

Among Mitch's hallmark achievements are his spectacular reclaimed stump thrones. He didn't craft them in his studio, but rather chainsaw-sculpted them on site. Like many towns and villages who lost their magnificent American elm trees to the Dutch elm disease, so has Cambridge, Mass., where Mitch lives. But instead of felling the dead or dying trees, uprooting root bases from the sidewalks and turning it all into mulch, Cambridge took a different approach.

With support from the city government, the town arborists left a few remaining elm stumps on along sidewalks, and commissioned Mitch to exercise his artistic talent to craft thrones and street chairs out of them. He used chainsaws, angle grinders, adzes, axes, rasps and files, and over the years created several artistic seats. Much of his civic furniture is of substantial width and height, so steps had to be carved out in some to give curious pedestrians an opportunity to climb up and check them out.

Mitch told me that from the inception of this project everyone knew that his thrones would not last forever, but what actually does? Since these organic pieces have real roots in the ground and are subject to sun, rain, snow and ice, the reality is that they will eventually deteriorate.

To ensure long-term preservation of tree trunks and root bases like these you'd need to fully detach them from the elements, but perhaps most importantly from water and oxygen. Depending on the specie, non-living trees rooted in the soil will not keep their structural integrity for more than a decade

BEFORE AND AFTER

In 2012 Mitch was commissioned to give a second chance to a dead red oak tree, which was rooted in a playground on the banks of the Charles River. When the tree was still alive it shaded a steel bench that engulfed it. Mitch thought that the elegant bench should remain and that the newborn tree should include a wooden canopy to shade the bench just as the tree had.

To extend the life span of the tree trunk sculpture and its limbs, Mitch capped the crosscut top of the tree and the end of the horizontal limb with copper cladding. This increases the tree's resistance to decay by preventing rain and snow from penetrating the tree from above. Mitch carved the wooden cranes from yew. The tree is finished with an oil finish.

A stump throne on Clay St. in Cambridge incorporates a colorful paint scheme.

Because this stump on Trowbridge St. in Cambridge had a large opening on one side, Ryerson filled it in with back slats and a slatted seat to complete the stool sculpture.

or so. Even if protected with a strong finish on the above-ground portion, they'll still decay since the roots migrate water from the ground up.

On top of this, all the horizontal surfaces at the top of the stump are open-pore end grain, which absorbs rainwater causing the wood fibers to rot. Nevertheless, through vision, hard work and determination, Mitch built some fantastic thrones.

His achievement is unique, as it allowed local residents to continue enjoying and appreciating their trees, although in a different form, for a few more years before they completely saccumb to nature. Mitch's collection of stump thrones has received recognition as inspiring original, transient, reclaimed creations, grafted to the past and providing a successful platform for street art and one-of-a-kind designs.

PETERS VALLEY WALNUT BOWL

"PETERS VALLEY WALNUT BOWL" BY YOAV LIBERMAN (2015)
Walnut scrap, 3" x 7" x 21"
PHOTOGRAPH BY YOAV LIBERMAN

While teaching a woodworking class at Peters Valley School of Craft in Layton, N.J., I had some time to work on a few new projects of my own, including this walnut bowl. In my work I'm often inspired by an abandoned block of wood, a tossed-away furniture piece or a found piece of hardware that sparks an idea to transform or incorporate it into a new project. Such was the case here. That all began when I noticed an odd-shaped piece of walnut in the woodshop's scrap bin.

The piece had long triangular proportions with a distinct lip-like apex. The lip was reminiscent of a limb branching out from the tree trunk that had been cut or broken off at some point, and then gradually closed off, although not completely. That area looked organic and intriguing – perhaps even

sensual – so I decided to transform the scrap into something new, hinging on the lip as an inspiration. I held the piece in my hand and contemplated what to do. Very soon it came to me that I want to turn it into a vessel, to carve out much of the center so the lip area became the focal point.

I began by marking with white chalk the area that determined the vessel's "waterline" – where the hull of a ship meets the surface of the water or, in this case, the surface of the table.

Following this, I cut the waterline with a bandsaw then

Pencil rendering of the
bowl's natural edge
and its waterline.

Wat er line

Outlining the waterline with white chalk.

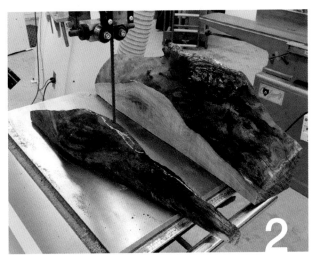

Sawing off the bowl's base at the waterline.

Jointing the waterline.

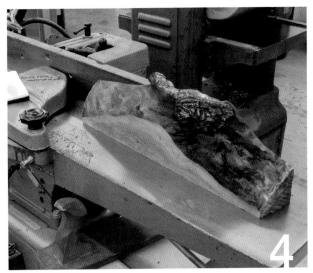

With the waterline flat, the bowl's long edge is jointed at 80°.

With the block secured with clamps and wooden cauls, carving begins at the middle of the outlined area.

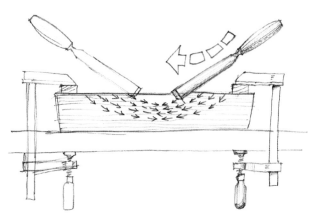

In this rendering, you can see how the carving gradually enlarges both the surface and depth of the hollow opening.

With a sharp gouge it's easy to carve across the grain too.

The deepening excavation calls for changing chisels to accommodate the bottom curve.

The finished walnut bowl and the gouges used to make it.

jointed it, as well as the long right-angle edge of the block, at an angle of 80°, to give it a more graceful ascent.

After this, I outlined the area I wanted to excavate and began gouging out the waste with a wide #8 sweep carving gouge.

I started at the middle of the outline and gradually enlarged both the surface of the excavation and its depth. Carving along the grain was fast and easy, but since my gouge was very sharp I had no problems gouging across the grain from the left and right as needed.

As my basin became steeper and steeper, I had to reach for a spoon gouge to help at the very bottom. I also tried a #7 gouge, but found that a #8 is better for the job because its corners tended to catch less on the excavation slopes. I had to reposition the clamps and cauls a few times to get into all

parts of the excavation. Because the bowl is elongated, and its bottom (the waterline) is long and flat, this wasn't a problem.

In the end, once carving away most of the wood as intended I let the bowl acclimate to our house to finish its drying period, which slightly affected the shape. After checking its moisture content I needed to re-joint the waterline for flatness, followed by some final gouge work to the hull. Finally, I applied some flax oil as a final step, then put a checkmark on this project.

If you have unusual scrap pieces, consider turning them into artistic bowls, spoons or cutting boards. A project like this is a fantastic opportunity to hone your carving skills and transform a rejected piece of wood into an artistic eye-catcher.

MAKER'S STORIES
Nancy Hiller

Inspired by architecture and furnishings from the late 19th-through the mid-20th century, Nancy Hiller designs and builds furniture and cabinetry with a strong period sensibility. With formal training and more than 30 years of professional experience as a designer/builder of furniture and cabinetry, she draws on a variety of techniques to produce projects that are highly customized in both design and craftsmanship.

Nancy has gained a reputation as a furniture design historian and educator whose affinity is with both the English and American Arts-and-Crafts movements. As a maker/scholar and as a towering figure in her field, Hiller is a celebrated author of a few books on woodworking and furniture design, and a prolific contributor to magazines and Internet publications worldwide.

Hiller designed and built Corona Plumosa as part of a project funded by a grant from Indiana University's Arts-Week 2012. Corona Plumosa is a riff on the 1927 "Spanish Renaissance Dining Set" produced by the Showers Brothers Furniture Company of Bloomington, Ind. The piece is made with quartersawn red oak from a storm-felled municipal tree, obtained through the City of Bloomington's "No Tree Left Behind" program through the Office of the Urban Forester, burly silver maple from a local forester, and black walnut from family property. The fretwork in the door is cut out of a sheet of 1/8" high-density fiberboard packing material from a local veneer plant that usually discards the packing material after it has been used. The door and drawer pulls are salvaged.

"TABULA MAXIMA" BY NANCY R. HILLER,
NR HILLER DESIGN, INC. (2014)
Oak, salvaged hinges, metal straps, 36" x 60" x 17"
PHOTOGRAPH BY KENDALL REEVES, SPECTRUM STUDIO. STRAP HARDWARE
MADE BY ADAM NAHAS, CYCLOPS STUDIO.

Sometimes a tree just has to go. When a client in the North Chicago suburb of Kenilworth decided to add to her 1912 Prairie-style house, she realized she'd have to fell a statuesque oak in the backyard. Nancy had the tree sawn and kiln-dried by Horigan Urban Forest Products of nearby Skokie, Ill., and gave it new life as flooring and the coffee table seen above. Nancy designed the table in conversation with her client, who wanted something large and sturdy with pull-out surfaces for casual dining in her family room. Aside from the swing-out shelves and the internal structure supporting them, the table is made entirely from the property's native tree. The butt hinges are salvaged.

Custom designed for the Ivy Tech John Waldron Arts Center in Bloomington, Ind., the reception desk seen on the next page is built throughout from locally grown and salvaged lumber. The panels are made from discarded quartersawn oak veneer backer boards; the counter is quartersawn red oak from a storm-felled tree that grew in Seminary Park, original site of Indiana University, and obtained through the City of Bloomington's "No Tree Left Behind" program through the Office of the Urban Forester.

"CORONA PLUMOSA" BY NANCY R. HILLER,
NR HILLER DESIGN, INC. (2012)
Quartersawn red oak, burly silver maple, black walnut, high-density fiberboard, salvaged hardware, 18½" x 27½" x 66¼"
PHOTOGRAPH BY KENDALL REEVES, SPECTRUM STUDIO

"IVY TECH DESK" BY NANCY R. HILLER, NR HILLER DESIGN, INC. (2011)
Quartersawn red oak, 60" x 156" x 42"
PHOTOGRAPH BY KENDALL REEVES, SPECTRUM STUDIO

In its basic appearance (though not in its internal accoutrements), Hoosier 2010 is a close reproduction of an antique "Napanee Dutch Kitchenet" from the early 20th century. In keeping with her wish to make the cabinet from local materials, Nancy crafted the piece with elm from a tree cut down to make room for the City of Bloomington Animal Shelter, and was made available through Bloomington's "No Tree Left Behind" recovery program. Like the wood, the limestone is also local and came from south-central Indiana, a major source of limestone for the construction industry. Its natural light-gray color has been darkened with a suspension of black powdered dye mixed in water, then sealed with an application of food grade mineral oil.

"HOOSIER 2010" BY NANCY R. HILLER, NR HILLER DESIGN, INC. (2009)
Salvaged elm, brass, tinted limestone, canvas, 24" x 40" x 66"
PHOTOGRAPH BY KENDALL REEVES, SPECTRUM STUDIO

CHAPTER 6

Restoring Reclaimed Hardware
The nuts and bolts of making hardware new again

From the time I began collecting reclaimed wood I remember salvaging all kinds of hardware pieces. I like to dismantle hardware from found furniture that is either too damaged or too big to haul back home, or impossible to take apart and lift from the street. This hardware sometimes includes handles and locks, latches and casters, and occasionally even ornamentation worthy of saving. And remember, most items left out on the curb the eve before trash day ends up in the landfill. So, why not save the hardware if you cannot save the furniture?

Over the years I became finicky about the types and quality of hardware I chose to salvage. Where in the past I used to save die-cast zinc and stamped-steel hardware, these days I mainly save stainless steel, cast iron, brass and bronze parts. I am not intimidated by hardware that displays an unattractive surface, or is painted or tarnished, as I know that can easily be rectified.

The best pieces of hardware are made from solid stainless steel, bronze or brass. Stainless steel is an alloy containing a percentage of chrome and nickel to negate corrosion, while brass and bronze are corrosion-resistant alloys based on copper. Painted, oxidized, bruised, scratched or patinated solid bronze or brass, and tarnished stainless steel hardware can be restored, literally, with flying colors. By rubbing with fine steel wool or an abrasive pad, followed by a polishing compound, it's possible to eliminate patina and past trauma to bring the items back to their original condition.

On the other hand, die-cast zinc hardware with its very thin copper, nickel or brass coating is more difficult to restore and structurally less reliable. Like die-cast zinc, stamped-steel hardware is also coated with a thin decorative protective layer

A simple keychain multi-tool will help you disconnect found hardware that is worthy of salvation.

that can be very delicate. In both coated-steel and die-cast hardware, surface scratches and a humid environment can lead to corrosion of the core material. This will progress the deterioration of the top coating, which eventually flakes off. This reality limits the restorative qualities of this hardware.

In cases where coated hardware is covered with grime and light surface scratches you can try to polish them back to the original factory sheen with a polishing compound or very fine steel wool. But as I mentioned before, if some of the coating has already flaked off or if the coating is very thin and brittle, you run the risk of over-polishing and exposing the core material even further.

The key to whether a hardware item is worth working with is identifying what kind of hardware you've reclaimed.

Ferrous or nonferrous? Even if you can't tell, a magnet can.

HARDWARE, HARDWARE EVERYWHERE

My friend Shay Avrahami has a healthy obsession for collecting and restoring pieces of worthy hardware he finds abandoned on the street, in Dumpsters or on deserted furniture awaiting the garbage truck. When he sees an old apartment undergoing renovation, he makes a mental note and remembers to revisit the site occasionally to see if the renovators have trashed old doors, windows or, sadly, antique furniture. If he can't save the furniture (unfortunately he can't host too many items in his tiny place) he will at least save the valuable knobs, handles, latches, locks and other items he believes that at some point, via karma or luck, he could put back to good use while doing what he loves the most – restoring old furniture.

Ferrous metal or not?

Hardware made of cast iron, steel, and stainless steel alloys are mostly made of iron, and will attract a magnet. Die-cast zinc, brass, copper and bronze do not contain iron and won't lure a magnet.

My first step in trying to identify between these two families of hardware is to use a magnet as a "sniffing dog." If the magnet adheres to the hardware piece you know that it's predominantly made of steel or iron. If magnetic hardware looks silvery or yellowish it means that it has been plated with nickel or brass. If a hardware piece doesn't attract a magnet, it means that it belongs to the non-ferrous family.

With experience, you should be able to differentiate between stainless steel and nickel-plated steel hardware. If you're not sure, try to file a spot on a hidden surface on the hardware and see if the piece's core presents a different material color than the surface. Stainless-steel hardware has the same material all through; steel-plated nickel, on the other hand, will expose subtle changes in appearance of the core material.

Lightly sanding a spot on the underside reveals hardware's true identity: The silver shine of the piece on the left indicates brass-plated die-cast metal, while the golden hue on the right signifies sold brass.

Is it brass, bronze or die-cast?

If your hardware did not react to the magnets (and it's not obviously plastic) it's either brass, bronze or die-cast zinc. Turn your hardware over, such as in the case of a concealed handle, and look at the threads that accept the mounting screws. If the threads look silvery it means that the core material is most likely die-cast zinc. Die-cast zinc is a silvery alloy made predominantly from zinc and is more brittle than brass or bronze.

If you're not sure, you can verify the nature of the hardware by filing or sanding away the topcoat on a hidden spot to try to reach the core material. If the core material is silvery it's definitely die-cast zinc. Many brass hardware pieces are coated with nickel or chrome, which gives them a silvery tone on the outside. If you're not positive whether they are plated die-cast zinc or brass do the filing test. If the exposed core material is golden-hued, the piece is solid brass.

From a powered rotary tool and chemical cleaners, to simple picks and brushes, cleaning reclaimed hardware is often a matter of using whatever works.

From top: A tarnished brass drawer pull; the brass shine starts to show through with light buffing; thoroughly cleaned, the brass pull almost looks brand new.

A rotary tool outfitted with a sanding wheel or wire brush removes buildup quickly.

Removing fossilized paint, varnish and tarnish from hardware

Salvaged hardware, even if made of corrosive-resistant materials such as bronze and brass, is almost always covered with oxidation (patina), accumulated grime or, in the worst cases, it's painted over a few times.

Sometimes patinated hardware is exactly what you want for a newly designed project. In this case I recommend cleaning the grime and dirt off by lightly scrubbing the item with 0000 steel wool moistened with mineral spirits. Then moisten a cotton cloth or paper towel with mineral spirits, and wipe the hardware clean of any residue left by the steel wool.

Removing patina

If you'd like to achieve a polished look, use a more aggressive steel wool, abrasive pad or even a high-speed rotary tool equipped with an abrasive disc or brush. Then, once the patina has been removed you can decide what level of polish you want for the new/old surface. By using finer and finer abrasives or polishing compounds you will be able to reach a very high level of sheen.

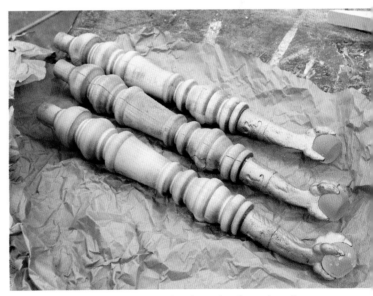

Painted or varnished hardware

If your hardware item is painted over or is covered with old protective lacquer that looks unattractive, I recommend using paint stripper to entirely remove the old finish.

Apply the stripper to the surface and let it soften the layers of finish.

Then use any combination of a scraper, steel brush and/or picks remove the old paint or varnish.

If your stripper can be rinsed off with water, then dunk the item in soapy water.

Scrub with steel wool or an abrasive pad.

When thoroughly cleaned, rinse in water and dry it with a hair dryer or a paper towel. The difference with the original look is like night and day.

Removal of patina, paint and rust with sand blasting

An effective, albeit aggressive, way of removing surface contaminants and irregularity from hardware items is to blast the surface with high-speed abrasive particles. Sandblasting can rapidly cut the stripping time and allow you to avoid the use of chemical strippers. Take into account that this technique is very aggressive and that prolonged unintended exposure of the surface to the particle jet could result in a pitted surface.

Sandblasting removes rust fast and deep, but also erodes other surfaces if you don't mask them off. The author sandblasted these piano stool legs to remove rust from the talon feet and strip finish from the wood at the same time. The unmasked glass balls turned etched-gray with the sandblasting.

Rust removal from ferrous hardware

Rust, the mortal enemy of steel and iron, can be removed via a few techniques. You can erode it with abrasives and steel brushes, you can use chemicals or acids, you can submerge rusted objects in a bath of sodium carbonate (also known as "washing soda") and water, and with the help of electricity reverse the corrosion through a process known as electrolysis. And if this is not enough, I have recently learned about a cutting edge technology that utilizes laser beams to incinerate rust away. Which method is best for your application? It depends on the object, the amount of rust on it and how much time you want to invest to remove it.

Submerged in vinegar

Which method to choose?

To remove rust from garden tools, sheet metal, steel furniture, wrought iron and simple hardware pieces I would use sandpaper, abrasive pads or sandblasting. Whenever I'm dealing with intricate shapes, delicate ornamentations, objects that have threads (such as nuts and bolts), precision measuring tools and cutting tools I choose the chemical way.

The former is an aggressive and rapid removal technique. It not only eliminates the rust, but if you're not careful it can erode steel and iron surfaces around it, as abrasive media tends to round over corners and dull edges. In contrast to the abrasive approach, removing rust via a chemical reaction is a slower process that affects only the rusted areas, leaving the rest of the surface mostly untouched.

Removing rust with a rotary tool

Another option for removing rust fast with moderate control on the abrasive medium is using a rotary tool such as "Dremel." It may give you more control to sand off stubborn pitting and high spots. A small rotary tool is perfect for intricate detail on hardware elements, and can accept tiny brushes, sanding pads, sanding flaps and disks. With a steady hand and protected by a respirator and goggles, you can achieve quite a lot. However, pay attention not to over-sand, as you run the risk of removing good metal and not just

corrosion.

Techniques I almost never use

Revolving steel or brass brushes, flap sanders and fiber abrasive disks – which many use for removing patina and rust from railings, wrought iron and flat surfaces – can be fast and partially effective, but are noisy and aggressive. Revolving steel and brass brushes mounted on an angle grinder or drill may remove rust, but most likely only the loose and flaky particles on easy-to-access areas. Sanding and grinding discs are much more effective than brushes, but are highly aggressive. They, too, are not recommended for removing rust from delicate details or valuable tools or items.

Removing rust with chemicals

In my experience there are two main options: acids and dedicated pH-neutral rust-removing chemicals. Over the years I've experimented with 5% vinegar, 20% vinegar, citric acid solutions and a product called Evapo-Rust. Among the four, Evapo-Rust, and other commercial products of its kind such as Rust-Oleum Rust Dissolver are the only ones with a neutral pH level. That means that they only work on the

A baking soda bath neutralizes the acid.

A final rinse.

rust, and that you don't have to worry about neutralizing acid residues possibly left on the surfaces after the removal process. You just need to wash with water and dry the objects.

If you choose to use acids, many recommend neutralizing the treated surface (after scrubbing the rust off and washing it) via a secondary immersion of the object in a solution of baking soda followed with a secondary rinse.

Before subjecting an object to acids or chemicals make an effort to wash and scrub away any traces of oil and loose rust with a dish soap solution and stiff brush.

Vinegar

Regular 5% vinegar (the food-grade type you buy at the grocery store) is probably the cheapest and the most available means for removing rust. Instead of 5% vinegar you can use stronger 20% vinegar. You won't find 20% vinegar at the grocery, however, as it's typically known as "cleaning vinegar." It's usually sold in home improvement stores and online. Using 20% vinegar gives you the same results as food-grade vinegar, but faster.

Fill a plastic or glass container with vinegar, then submerge the object and let the vinegar do its job. Check the

de-rusting progress and scrape loose rust off with a brass or steel brush or use steel wool or an abrasive pad. Mechanically removing the loose rust encourages the chemical reaction to access the remaining surface rust.

After a few hours of immersion, check the progression of the de-rusting process and remove additional loose rust with a stiff brush, steel wool, picks, hooks or a scraper. Then immerse the object again as necessary. Depending on the amount of rust on the object and the concentration of the vinegar you use, you might need to immerse the object in the solution as little as a few hours, or up to a day or more.

When the vinegar has affected most of the rust, buff off the black patina that formed on the metal during the process using a cloth or a very fine polishing media (very fine steel wool can work too).

After the metal is free of corrosion, rinse it with water and neutralize the acidic vinegar in a solution of a baking soda and water. One teaspoon per cup of water is fine.

Give the hardware a final rinse in water again, and then dry immediately – you'd be surprised just how quickly rust can re-form on damp, bare metal. You can use paper towels followed by an air blower (or even a hair dryer) and when that

Supplies for making your own citric acid

is done apply a protective coat to the surface such as gun blue, wax, paint, or lacquer to prevent rust from reoccurring

Citric acid

You can make your own citric acid from a powder available online and in some stores. I dilute one volume unit of citric acid in 10 volume units of water, which gives an approximate pH level higher than 20% vinegar, around pH 1.5. And if we mixed citric acid in less water we could create an even more potent acidic solution. By the way, it's possible to buy vinegar at 30% concentration on Amazon.com and other online stores.

There are situations where you can't, or do not want, to immerse an object in acid or other rust-removal solution. For instance, in some cases I might not be able to find a container that's physically large enough to hold the object. Other times, the rust may only be in a few spots and there's no reason to subject the entire object to acid. In these cases I use a jelly-like rust remover such as Naval Jelly, which allows me to confine

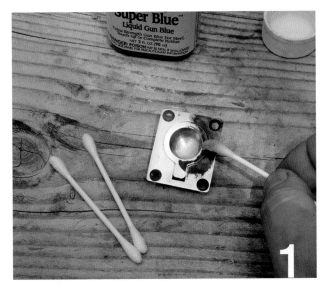

the rust removal to the affected areas. The application is much the same. You smear the jelly on the rust and wait until it does its magic.

Quick re-patination of polished hardware

If you want to bestow your reclaimed hardware with an antique appearance or a very dark look consider using the gun blue family of products. Once the fluid is applied on a grease- and oil-free surface, it turns the surface dark. The more you apply, the darker it becomes.

Using cotton Q-tips, apply gun blue on an oil-free brass or bronze surface, and wait until it stops darkening.

Once you like the new look, rinse the piece in water and lightly polish with a cotton rag.

Use 0000 steel wool to buff off the surface if you want to lighten the dark patina.

In photo 4 you can see three different surface treatments for brass: Dark brown patina, patinated-luster and polished.

Take into account that the newly created patina is thin and can be scratched or even rubbed off easily. To protect it for years to come, polish the surface lightly with a cotton rag or a paper towel, followed by a coat of wax or, even better, varnish or lacquer. If you wish to achieve a look of a patinat-

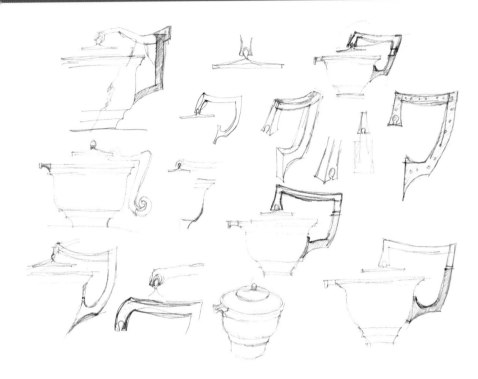

Brainstorming design ideas.

Does "reclaiming the reclaimed," sound redundant? Well, in the case of the Flash Teapot it actually happened. It's a reclaiming story with an interesting twist. Most reclaim artists and craftspeople that I know have reclaimed their own scraps in one way or the other, but with this project the reclaiming occurred twice.

It all began on an early spring visit to the Harvard Museum of Natural History. Approaching the museum I noticed a pile of fallen tree limbs near an old and frail maple tree. The limbs showed evidence of decay, which explained why they had been pruned. I immediately wanted to turn them into something special.

"FLASH TEAPOT" BY YOAV LIBERMAN (2005)
Maple, walnut, copper, brass, tinted epoxy, found camera flash
9" x 7" x 9"
PHOTOGRAPH BY YOAV LIBERMAN

One of the branches became a decorative art piece in the shape of a teapot, although not immediately. The piece started out as a half-spherical bowl with a coved base, but while finishing it up it tragically broke into many pieces. Disappointed and saddened, I collected the pieces, but instead of discarding them I decided to keep them; perhaps down the road they could be of some use.

For two years they collected dust on a shelf in my studio until I received, and accepted, an invitation to build a teapot for "The Teapot Redefined" show at Mobilia Gallery in Cambridge, Mass. I knew instantly that my broken bowl had finally found its true calling.

After sketching a few options I came up with a proposal that included the broken bowl, mended with the same technique archaeologists use to fix broken ancient ceramic, but with a copper and walnut handle and a lid. In the spirit of using reclaimed materials, I recalled that I once found an

Using epoxy to reassemble the shards of the original bowl.

Forming the handle.

orphaned silver lid, which most likely used to crown a sugar container. After a few more sketches, a scale drawing emerged outlining the design, including the found lid. I presented the idea to the gallery and received their approval.

First, I glued together the remains of the shattered wood bowl using black epoxy in an effort to highlight the mend in juxtaposition to the original wood.

Then, I made the base of the teapot handle arm from a lamination of claro walnut and veneer.

To add lightness and elegance to the arm I asked my friend and frequent collaborator, metal artist Leslie Hartwell, to create a copper and brass cantilever girder-like extension from which the lid could be suspended. After all the pieces were assembled I hung the silver lid by the handle arm, boxed up the teapot and took it to the gallery. What followed was a unique chain of events that I could have not anticipated.

The gallery owner looked at the teapot and seemed sur-

prised, explaining that she expected a bigger lid than the one I produced. She encouraged me to try and see if I could change it or increase its size.

Quite honestly, my first urge was to fiercely defend my artistic vision. But, I gave it some thought and decided to swallow my pride and make an effort to empathize with her reaction. Coincidentally, on my way home I noticed a "Free Stuff" box on the side of the street. The box contained old photography equipment and other trinkets. The item that really caught my eye was an old camera flash, the kind that opens up into a dome shape.

At that moment a figurative light bulb flashed in my mind, and I knew that this flash was a Godsend – the perfect lid for my teapot. To incorporate it into the piece I turned a walnut finial that acted both as a hub and hanging knob for the new lid. The lid can be taken in and out of the handle arm, while the knob allows the reflector to open and close.

Adding metalwork to the teapot handle.

Vintage Honeywell "Tilt-A-Mite" camera flash.

When I revealed the new-and-improved teapot to the gallery owner, she positively glowed. We both were enthusiastic about the look intrinsic to the new alteration. For me it was an important lesson: Even after years of studying and practicing my art, it is wise to be open to constructive criticism, especially if you want to have a fruitful relationship with gallery owners and clients.

After the Mobilia show ended the teapot traveled to SOFA Chicago for display. When that show closed I sent the teapot to Del Mano gallery in Los Angeles. There it was spotted by Gloria and Sonny Kamm, the renowned teapot collectors, who acquired it for their collection.

It was a long journey but one that was worth taking, for sure.

Removed and cleaned, the flash reflector is fitted with a walnut finial for hanging.

CHAPTER 7

Designing with Reclaimed Wood
A series of negotiations

Working with reclaimed wood can be an invigorating and challenging experience that forces us to negotiate in the most fundamental way between form and function, and aesthetics and meaning, to produce an outcome that can be quite spectacular.

Because of its intrinsic richness, diversity and versatility, reclaimed wood is a wonderful material to design with. And the fact that it comes charged with so much physical and inspirational potential makes it an exciting canvas that will complement furniture and dwelling spaces.

However, some reclaimed wood peculiarities can be finicky to work with and deserve attention. The number one constraint with many types of reclaimed wood is the physical dimensions of the reclaimed "building blocks" we have to work with. This is the case when working with small Recycled/Scrapped pieces, found reclaimed, and some Heritage Reclaimed. Yet, as we often see, resource limitations and material constraints can be the perfect generators of an honest and elegant synthesis of design ideas.

Thus, it is important to consider a design approach that takes into account the predispositions of the type, size and condition of the reclaimed wood you've obtained or are willing to acquire. By carefully evaluating reclaimed wood's unique hallmarks, plus others factors I'll cover in this chapter, we'll be able chart the right course for a successful project.

▲ As discussed earlier, some reclaimed wood is available in sizes not drastically different from the nominal dimensions of new lumber. Massive timbers can be sold as-is, or be resawn into boards of substantial length, width and thickness. This offers a blank canvas to draw upon and presents considerable design possibilities.

◄ Working with large reclaimed wood elements is a liberating experience almost devoid of any constraints. This exceptionally long dining table, designed by Erica Diskin, is at the Ledger Restaurant in Salem, Mass.
MICHAEL DISKIN

The Venture Cafe at the Cambridge Innovation Center at One Broadway, Cambridge, Mass. To achieve this attractive look, Irene Ferris used reclaimed barnboard from Longleaf Lumber, combined with newly milled Southern yellow Pine.

MICHAEL FITZHENRY

Design approaches based on the reclaimed surface and core

Many reclaimed materials are like an archaeological excavation: The deeper you dig, the more profound is the change in appearance from the surface of the wood. Therefore, we need to think about how much, if any, original wood surface we want to skim off, and what kind of relationship we want to form between the reclaimed wood and other elements in the new piece. Here are a few possibilities:

Reclaimed in the raw

Using raw reclaimed as-is throughout the entire piece or in selected areas. Showing patina, distorted and distressed (or even intentionally crude) surfaces on the new furniture.

Treated reclaimed

When reclaimed wood receives some surface alterations such as light sanding or hand planing, a protective finish, etc. As part of the original patina and surface erosion gets smoothed out, the wood appears "cleaner," yet it still conveys its reclaimed heritage.

Pristine-core reclaimed

In this case the piece or project is made using reclaimed wood's core beauty without showing any, or very little, evidence of past use and patina, such as hardware and fastener holes.

Reductive reclaimed or transitional reclaimed

This approach is commonly used with Salvaged/Recovered timber or logs, where the maker reduces the volume of the raw reclaimed and transforms it into something else, leaving behind traces of the original material. The new piece seems as if it organically morphed or emerged out of the salvaged wood. Many pieces of Reductive/Transitional reclaimed tend to be on the sculptural spectrum of woodworking.

Contrasting reclaimed or reclaimed juxtaposition

In this case the reclaimed elements are juxtaposed with new wood, painted wood or a completely different material recruited to highlight the reclaimed components or participate as an equal partner in the new piece's composition.

Designer Gilad Erjaz created this stunning entrance door from lightly sanded oak floorboards from decommissioned boxcars.

MOSHI GITELIS

The author's "Mulberry Trio" (featured at the end of this chapter) juxtaposes paint, hardware and natural wood grain.

▲ The author's "Six Pack" modular chest is an example of pristine-core reclaimed wood.

For sculptor Peter Strasser, studying the raw timber and setting the tree to the exact angle and pitch takes more consideration than actually making the reductive cuts. An example of reductive reclaimed, these "Standing Tall" sculptures appeared at the Katherine Konner Sculpture Park at the Rockland Center for the Arts in West Nyack, N.Y. ▶

DEAN POWELL

PETER STRASSER

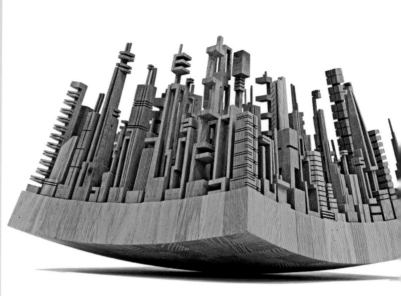

THE CITYSCAPE WOODWORKER

James McNabb is a brilliant young sculptor/designer based in Philadelphia. McNabb produces one-of-a-kind cityscape-inspired wood sculptures that explore the limitless possibilities of the urban landscape and our human relationship to it. McNabb uses discarded pieces of wood to create sculptures, some with unique and alluring characteristics that are contextualized to draw new meaning out of the material and encourage viewers to create their own perspectives of the urban landscape.

McNabb blends traditional and experimental woodworking using a band saw much as an artist uses a brush. This intuitive method allows him to generate forms rapidly, working through new and exciting ideas without preliminary design development. The resulting works are distorted compositions of abstracted architectural forms.

When he exhausts the possibilities of finding materials he turns to his father for help. Gary McNabb locates local municipal felled trees, which he mills and dries before delivering them to his son's studio. The lumber for this spectacular "Walnut City Wheel" project was processed by McNabb's father from a tree that fell in their New Jersey hometown.

Design approaches based on the reclaimed physical size

Much of the recognition that reclaimed wood pieces receive stems from furniture and decorative arts pieces that are made from a compilation of smaller reclaimed building blocks joined together to make the new.

It is obvious to anyone who has worked or considered working with reclaimed materials, that the size of the original finds may not suffice for building whole or even part of a new piece. Those who work with reclaimed wood often have to connect or glue together smaller reclaimed building blocks in order to obtain the necessary dimension required for the new design. For example, if you like to work with reclaimed pallet wood, and plan to build a tabletop from it, you are faced with the reality that most pallets boards don't exceed 36" in length. If your tabletop length needs to be, say, 60", you have to figure out a way to connect shorter pieces in a way that will be both structurally sound and visually attractive.

▲ Peit Hein Eek of The Netherlands created "Afval Kast in Sloopout" ("Waste Cabinet in Scrapwood") from dozens of mismatched and oddly shaped scraps.

▼ This scarf joint creates a long beam from two short ones. The intricate pegged construction is very strong and is also aesthetically pleasing.

Quilt making – designing big, with small building blocks

I use the name "Reclaimed Quilt" to describe the ensemble of secondary, miscellaneous, small or odd-shaped segments and scraps merged to create a tapestry or quilt that provides the basis for the new piece.

Since the beginning of civilization, makers have been combining small leftovers such as reclaimed leather, fabric and metal pieces to make bigger "canvases" from which clothes, household items and tools were made. Carpenters who needed to provide long beams in situations where their logs were just too short developed reliable techniques to join beams in order to make longer ones. These honest approaches, born from scarcity and necessity, influence and inspire us when creating a new woodworking project from smaller reclaimed entities.

Structural considerations for making a wooden quilt

Before designing a pattern for connecting secondary pieces of wood together we need to identify what kind of load the part(s) in the project built from the quilt will have to withstand. For

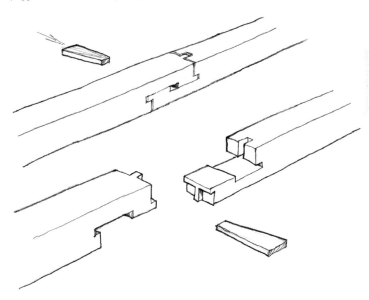

example, let's take a table to help us understand the type of loads and forces acting on each of the components, and which one of them will be subjected to the lion's share of the stresses.

Designing with Reclaimed Wood **125**

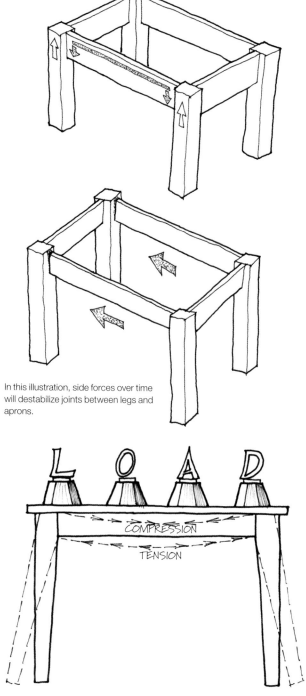

THE EFFECT IS CLEAR

Mustafa Gök is a Turkish designer/woodworker who works with reclaimed tree logs he salvages from the side of the road near his countryside studio. (The trees and logs were discarded, as they could not be utilized by the standard lumber industry.) Most are small in size, partially hollowed out by decay, twisted or deformed. Gök examines them and utilizes them to the best of their potential. Some are resawn into unique shaped planks that he later incorporates into furniture, where others – short logs – are used in their entirety, flanked by a transparent resin cast. The reclaimed resin pairing allows us to appreciate both the raw organic properties of the tree side by side with the modern translucent material, which on top of complementing the overall shape, provides a structural/functional counterbalance.

In this illustration, side forces over time will destabilize joints between legs and aprons.

Furniture structure 101

Our table has four legs, four aprons or beams, and one tabletop. Load is the weight and forces that act mainly on the tabletop. That consists of the weight of the top itself, plus the weight of items we put on it: heavy dishes during a meal, books, a computer, the weight of our arms when we lean on it, or even the weight of our entire body when we stand on it to replace a light bulb.

Some of the forces that act on the table and its top are applied by us, the users, as we dine on it or lean on it. Other

Load on the tabletop causes compression on the beams or aprons' top and tensions their bottoms. This illustration exaggeratedly demonstrates that under extreme load situations the legs will splay out

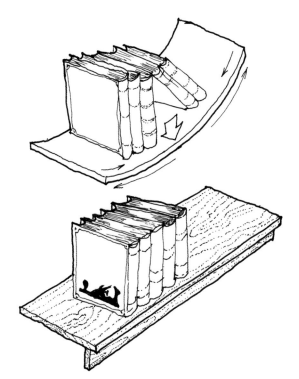

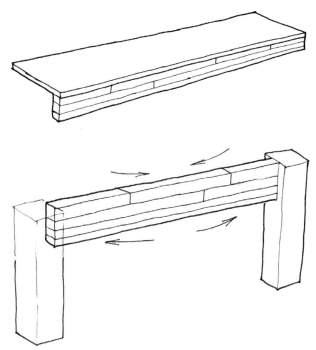

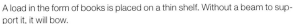

A load in the form of books is placed on a thin shelf. Without a beam to support it, it will bow.

Aligning the longest scraps of reclaimed wood at the bottom of the shelf's beam provide continuous grain in a critical part that needs to withhold considerable tension. As in the shelf illustration, structural beams such as in tables, bed rails and dressers made from scrap wood or short segments should include the longest elements at the bottom.

forces are accidental, such as a side push when we stumble against it, or by a cat that jumps on it and dives into a casserole bowl (it happened to me, and my cat survived this suicide mission). Most of these forces are generated via gravity and act vertically toward the ground, but some are applied sideways and over time can weaken the joints between the legs and the aprons.

The tabletop, as mentioned before, carries most of the load but it's spread along and across a lot of surface, so our quilted top can, in practice, be designed with more freedom and with smaller parts, as each one of them needs to handle a relatively small amount of load. From the top the load migrates down, and the whole weight of the tabletop and whatever's on it now rests on the four beams or aprons, which need to support it. The beams bend as result of the stresses applied by the load above. In effect, they behave much like floor joists, trusses, bridge girders or bed rails. They are among the most critical

elements in our structural design considerations, and they have to be built with care in order to withhold the weight applied on them.

Under load, the upper part of the beam is compressed, while the lower part is put under tension. Solid-wood aprons or beams perform very well as they are made homogeneously from long continuous grain. Their lower part behaves similarly to an uninterrupted rope or cable. But if the beam is made of smaller pieces the grain cannot have a continuum from one end to the other, which renders the segmented beam weaker.

The preferable way to compose segmented beams from secondary parts (a beam quilt) is to find the longest possible parts and align them at the bottom of the beam, while the shortest parts are laid out at the top. And if we can find scraps that are as long as the entire intended beam, that's even better. We also need to strive for long overlapping long-grain glue

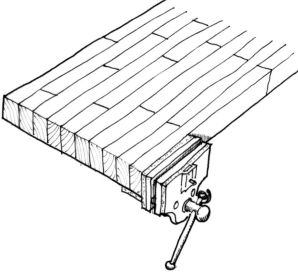

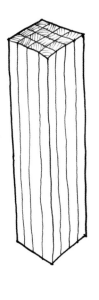

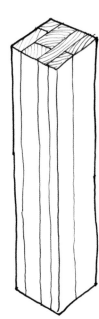

▲ Making a new wood quilt from many smaller pieces is a practical way to reuse reclaimed wood and scraps. If your quilt is thick enough, it will withstand a lot of load even without apron beams underneath. For this benchtop the author created a quilt made of random-length hardwood pallet rails.

◀ Legs comprising continuous-grain wood strips are more resilient to stresses and abuse than legs made from short segments. Furniture artist Jack Mauch built this table's legs from a "bundle" of glued-together thin strips of walnut. After gluing them together he shaped them into exquisite animal-like legs. The illustration shows how a glueup like this would work.

joints between secondary elements, as that helps the "little guys" to support each other. In woodworking, the joint between two end-grain components is recognized as a very weak joint that should be strengthened by an intermediate "match-maker" such as a floating tenon or a dowel. On the other hand, a long-grain to long-grain glue joint is much stronger.

Now, the load migrates from the beams down to the legs. Most of the time the legs will facilitate an uninterrupted flow toward the floor and will have to deal with only compression forces. Therefore, we can be somewhat less concerned about how to amalgamate the leg quilt. But if the legs' shape is complex, if they flare out, are extremely thin, or if the table may be subjected to occasionally disturbances such as kicking or movements, we might want to create the legs from a bundle of secondary elements made of the longest continuous grain we can find. This way, if tension forces come into play the legs

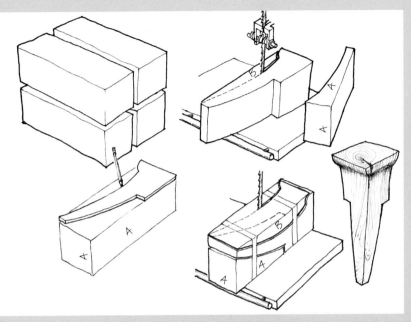

PATCHED TOGETHER

In the case of "Corduroy," a small stool/table I built in the early 2000s, I made use of short Douglas fir cutoffs reclaimed from the garbage of a local school. Facing the limited length of the beams I decided to design a piece made from four upright elements that would display the beautiful circular crosscut pattern on its top. Because each segment of the stool was thick and wide, I had to first cut its outline on the bandsaw and only then glue them together.

I began by making a pattern that was very helpful in tracing the design on the face of the beams. Following this, I cut the leg's curves on the band saw, and then temporarily reinstated the scraps that I just cut around the leg. Then I turned the beam/leg 90° and traced the outline of the other face. After sawing each leg for the second time, I glued everything together before rasping and sanding the stool to refine the details and eliminate the band saw marks. The finishing touch is a few coats of polyurethane varnish.

will be able to mitigate them successfully.

Design ideas for making beams from short stock

Medium length or even long pieces of reclaimed wood can be joined together to make structural beams that are both strong and elegant. Our most important consideration is the appearance of the new beam rather than concerns for its structural integrity since, as mentioned above, by connecting enough overlapping elements, glued or joined with fasteners, we can create a very effective beam. Granted, this beam has to be thicker than a comparable beam made from solid wood, but this additional thickness won't be noticed in most furniture

and isn't a drawback.

The industrial or agrarian-looking joint.
Connecting the beams with thick overlapping plates, visual bolts, or glue and pegs will create a long beam that looks rustic and robust. Use this solution for furniture and interior design elements, or even new load-bearing structures that look industrial, historical and rural.

While making a tall bed for myself that would provide storage space underneath, I was not only limited by the length of the sub beams (rails) that I had to work with, but also by the stock that I was able to find for the legs. I came up with a way to connect short beams via an intermediate tongue glued

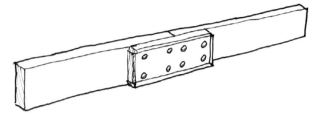

Joining beam segments with a simple plate.

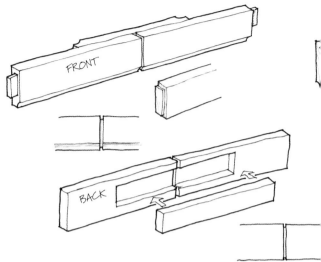

This illustration shows that the buttressing plate can either be glued and screwed over the two sub beams, or embedded in a wide channel between them.

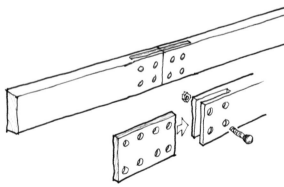

Joining beam segments with a hidden internal plate.

inside a groove in one of the beams, and nested into a mirroring groove in the other. To add rigidity to this construction I secured the joint with carriage bolts. Since my reclaimed leg stock was short, I had to come up with a solution for the two legs supporting the headrest. Remembering that I had in my collection two pneumatic chair back brackets, I decided to install them between the short headrest legs and the mattress rail/beam.

A take on this design that pushes it even further into the rustic realm can include an external plate to buttress the two beams.

A shadow line joint to divert the eyes from the transition.

If you are looking to make a beam that doesn't advertise the fact that it was, out of necessity, made of secondary pieces, consider creating a shallow groove at the location where the parts meet.

We can connect the subunits and support the joint (by adding a thick plate of wood at the back), but anyone looking at the beam will see the small seam defining the transition between each sub beam and its neighbor. Trying to paint the beam in order to hide the seam may work for some time, but after a while small changes in humidity and other natural causes will allow this seam to manifest to the surface and be visible on the paint job.

However, this visual disadvantage can be circumvented by adding a defined narrow, shallow groove at the location of the seam. The groove can be made in the shape of a rabbet or a shoulder on one end of a sub beam prior to gluing the entire beam, or it can be milled after the integration of the subunits into one long entity. The groove transforms the necessary and

In these illustrations we can see the effects of a shadow-line groove over a seam between two sub beams. The emphasized "borderline" groove is very effective in hiding any seam that develops in the varnish or paint after gluing the two end-grain edges together.

YOAV LIBERMAN

The author's "Louisa's Flat File" uses the shadow-line groove to disguise how the lower beam was pieced together and add a pleasing visual element.

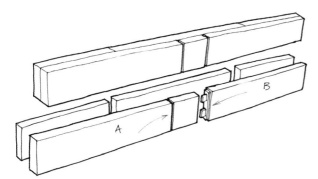

How the lower beam of "Louisa's Flat File" was constructed.

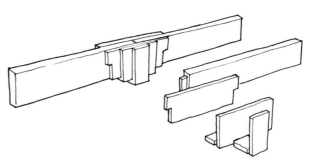

A detail focal point added in the middle of a composite beam both hides and visually enhances a beam joint.

mundane seam into a design statement. It creates a defined shadow line that paces the length of the beam with a darker line that camouflages any future micro seam that might develop in the varnish or the paint job. Shadow lines via moldings, grooves and rabbets are excellent ways to elegantly border transitions between surfaces, by diverting the eye from potential glue or installation inaccuracy, into what is perceived as a thoughtful design statement.

I used this technique to build a portable base for a flat-file storage case of drawers and table. To make the short rails for the piece's base I glued together two strips of scrap wood, long-edge to long-edge. And to make the rectilinear base's long rails, I relied on old reclaimed rails that I found on the street, and planned on reusing their existing tenons and bed bolt fasteners. I knew I had to shorten the rails by removing a segment from the middle then connect them with a plate, but a measuring mistake led me to cut the rails too short. My solution was to add a rail segment in between the two halves of the original rail, connecting the three parts end-grain to end-grain. These subunits had to be supported by a wood plate that I glued and screwed in between the end-grain joint. To hide the composite beam's double seam, I formed a rabbeted recess at both end-grain surfaces of the middle plate.

Hiding the transition by building up a detail focal point in the middle of the composite beam is a creative solution for incorporating reclaimed wood of limited length. The

Here, designer Gilad Erjaz glued strips of reclaimed wood edge-to-edge to make a lively heterogeneous tabletop.

For her "Converse Lovejoy Furniture Project," designer Irene Ferri used reclaimed white oak from the original piers at Lovejoy Wharf in Boston, Mass., to create a quilted top for this lounge table at the new world headquarters of Converse.

build-up detail can both physically strengthen the transition, and invite the eye to study and appreciate it as an intentional design detail.

Design ideas for surface quilts

You can build surface quilts for tabletops, doors, shelves, benches and chair seats – any application where you need a wide, long surface. You can create a harmonious quilt in which small pieces of wood of different species are glued in a thoughtful pattern. You can cut the pieces into identical sizes and create a regimental parquetry look. And you can orchestrate the parts into abstract formations or even graduations that stem from their colors, sizes or special proximities.

The quilt segment can vary in thickness, be cut into rectilinear shapes, trapezoid shapes, parallelogram shapes or even triangles. Crosscutting strips of reclaimed wood on a table saw or miter saw will give you the most accurate repeatable results. When you design a quilt, strive for long-grain to long-grain joints, but if your pattern calls for an end-grain to end-grain connection consider reinforcing this inferior joint

Above you can see a few patterns for successful quilt designs.

with splines, biscuits or tenons.

Building a quilt panel from a few subsurfaces is recommended when the size or the complexity of the pattern is greater than average. Gluing together small segmented units, then sawing them accurately into tile-shaped panels, and lastly connecting the tile together will make the whole quilt operation more manageable and less stressful than connecting

Designer Victoria Valencia used a "clandestine" pneumatic pin nailer and glue to affix the patinated reclaimed segments to the top of one of her latest pieces, and placed weights on top of the core reclaimed fir pieces while gluing the sections to the substrate.

In the case of this tabletop made by Gilad Erjaz, the reclaimed-wood veneer was glued not only on the surface of the substrate but also on the edges via a waterfall effect. It conveys an appearance of a solid wood board, thick and rich with patina. This design also alleviates complications from gluing thick reclaimed segments together and dealing later with expansion and contraction of the unified panel, common with solid-wood glueups embraced by a frame.

all the segments in one gluing session. Because of the heterogeneous nature of reclaimed-wood quilt work, the quilts are best surfaced using sharp hand planes, handheld sanders or a drum sander.

Reclaimed quilt over a substrate

A substrate is a stable and flat core material made typically of MDF or plywood, upon which thin segments of reclaimed wood are laid out in a geometric pattern. The pattern can look much like the solid quilt we talked about before, but because we're less concerned with structural and glueup constraints, a greater degree of design liberty is permitted. When making a quilt over a substrate our main concern is how to glue the wide surfaces of the segments over the substrate. We can press

them down with clamps, brads, veneer press or a vacuum bag.

Advantages of using a quilt over substrate

The first advantage is that you use less reclaimed wood to cover an equivalent panel surface. If our reclaimed wood is rare or unique, we can resaw it once or a few times and harvest from the initial reclaimed volume many more surface units than the original full thickness board could have yielded.

The second advantage is the relative ease of the glueup. Where in making solid reclaimed-wood quilts we had to put a lot of attention into preparing the edges of the segments, then carefully press them together to create a strong bond between them, in the case of the quilt veneer over a substrate

"Waste Waste Varnished Armchair" features a mosaic of hundreds of thin pieces of reclaimed wood. Each chair measures 23.6" x 25.2" x 29.9".

our main concern is the design. We should certainly try to make the joints or seams between the segments perfect, but if we accidentally create microscopic gaps, they won't jeopardize the strength of the entire quilt board, as the substrate is the responsible agent for the structural stability of the unified veneer quilt.

Reclaimed de la Reclaimed: The mosaic work of Peit Hein Eek

The Dutch designer/maker Peit Hein Eek is perhaps the most prolific, successful and renowned reclaimed-wood artist in the world. He works with a bounty of materials and all kinds of reclaimed woods. Among his hallmark achievements in recent years are pieces built from reclaimed mosaic quilt. These are pieces with surfaces made from small tiles of reclaimed wood matrixed together over a skeleton of substrate material. Hein Eek's mosaic tiles are the waste products of the reclaimed wood he uses when building his other furniture. He named the mosaic line "Waste Waste." But perhaps a more sublime name would fit better: "Reclaimed de la Reclaimed."

The project was born more than 10 years ago as a reaction to the remorse of having to throw away expansive reclaimed/ waste material, which was initially considered too labor-in-

"NYC Waste Waste Mirror Cabinet." The lighted cabinet measures 43.3" x 14.9" x 43.3".

A typical turning session turns out a variety of shapes and wood species.

Occasionally, Dawson adds metal details to her finished turnings.

Heather Dawson starts her petite projects by cutting too-small-to-use scraps of reclaimed wood into diminutive turning blanks like these.

PETITE RECLAIMED

Heather Dawson of Allston, Mass., is a promising young woodworker and woodturner who specializes in reclaiming small wood scraps and turning them into beautiful decorative objects, mostly vases and bowls. Her miniature creations are delicate, well proportioned and refined. Through her work she demonstrates how even the tiniest of scraps, those cutoffs that many of us don't even bother with and toss into the firewood bin, can be transformed into objects of reverence and value.

Dawson's design approach stems from the dimensions and proportions of the scraps she finds. She tries to maximize the potential of each piece by carefully preparing square stock, which she then mounts in a lathe for turning. Her smallest pieces are under 1" in diameter and around 1" high; her biggest are 2" diameter by 5" tall. Sometimes she adds color to her precious creations and other times she leaves their natural grain intact.

tensive to work with. As an avid reclaimer, Hein Eek tried to come up with a technique that allowed him to utilize this Reclaimed de la Reclaimed and build pieces with them that, although more time-consuming to build, will be unique enough, and consequently attractive and saleable. In his own words Hein Eek tells us, "As opposed to almost any other product, the waste products [projects] are made with the patience of a saint; quite a feat considering this is an age in

which time is a rare commodity for pretty much everyone."

In one of his most recent collections, presented first at the Rossana Orlandi Gallery during the Salone del Mobile 2017 in Milan, he presented a spectacular piece of furniture covered with a mosaic of reclaimed wood. In typical Hein Eek candor, flavored with playful sarcasm, he says, "Especially for the Salone and ultimately to meet Rossana's request, we have made a cabinet that almost nobody needs, so it's really

Designing with Reclaimed Wood **135**

Bedroom wall cladding with barn wood, designed by Gilad Erjaz.

Designer Chris Webb's bedroom wall cladding of select Heritage heart pine from The Goodwin Company. The lower cabinet is made with reclaimed cypress.

chic. The little cabinet is made from the worst pieces of the NYC water-tower wood. The whitened and crackled surface resembles the skin of a prehistoric reptile."

Yet, when looking at Hein Eek's beautiful mosaic pieces, the words "waste" or "worst" will surely dissipate and be replaced with "superior" and "sublime."

Reclaim Cladding

One of the ways to make use of reclaimed floorboards, sidings, clapboards and other thin boards is to apply the materials as cladding over a three-dimensional skeleton or carcase to form cubistic furniture. Here are a few examples:

Reclaimed wood is a popular go-to choice among interior designers and architects who want to accentuate a wall. Cladding a wall draws attention to it, defining it as a prime visual element, and is used often in new home construction as well as renovations. The cladded wall will be the most important wall in a room, or the wall that divides a house into two parts. This wall can be the staircase wall, which flows between the lower and upper floors, or a partition wall between common areas and bedrooms. Or it can be a corridor wall that leads through different spaces in a building.

When reclaimed wood isn't that attractive… paint it

When choosing Common Reclaimed wood or found furniture parts, we often need to take into account that this inexpensive, or even free, material might have little or no aesthetic value. Yet these unattractive reclaimed-wood components or structures can easily be transformed into beacons of attention with a simple layer of paint. Paint possesses the ability to homogenize an eclectic surface, becoming a strong design statement. The combination of painted wood surfaces, side by side with rich and striking live edge or Heritage Reclaimed elements can enhance and uplift almost any furniture or wooden object, turning it into an invigorating piece of timeless design.

Allowing reclaimed wood "patina" to come the fore

It's a fascinating question that I ask myself over and over again: Why am I, and so many other designers makers and clients, so attracted to the bruised, distorted, scarred, grayed and complex texture of reclaimed wood? Is it because we pay heed to its age? Perhaps it's because we admire its character, its perseverance, bravado and defiance with the elements? Do

SASHA FLIT

Sigal Hadida's reclaimed legs' bench is made from a slab of municipal felled eucalyptus tree, and many reclaimed furniture legs that she has repurposed. A common practice among reclaimers is to stash found furniture parts for future use. In the case of Sigal it was abandoned and tossed away furniture legs which she then connected via an under rail to the live edge slab. To unify the under world and juxtapose it from the live edge slab above she painted the legs white.

MOSHI GITELIS

Gilad Erjaz designed this built-in display case with reclaimed wood left, as closely as possible, in the state in which he found it.

As with the display case, the reclaimed wood Gilad Erjaz used in this kitchen cabinetry shows off a lifetime of previous use including fastener holes, original paint and even remnants of old joinery.

we like to invite the weathered wood into our homes so we can absorb and be reminded of the strong authentic power or nature and time? Or perhaps it is because there's a hidden masochistic element in us that sees beauty in the tormented?

Quite possibly there's no solid answer to this question, and each of us holds a personal reasoning for liking to work with or admire the patina of reclaimed wood.

For me, at least, being able to work with rugged reclaimed wood is both a privilege and a challenge. I am thrilled with the idea of designing with materials that bare an impressive spectrum of physical history on their surfaces. I am excited with the task of preserving and celebrating this resource's chronicles, and I love the idea of accommodating this precious organic, and often sensitive, media in my new creations.

PROJECT
ASCENT

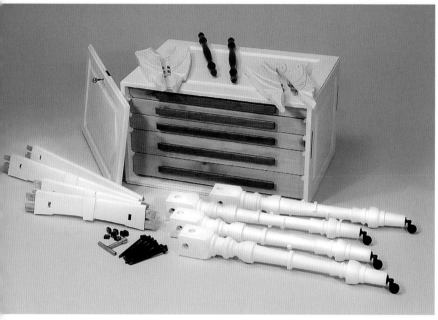

Discarded specimen trays.

"ASCENT" BY YOAV LIBERMAN

Reclaimed oak doors, reclaimed rubberwood legs, found pine specimen trays, reclaimed birch, walnut, brass, wenge, paint, 49" x 33" x 24"

PHOTOGRAPHS BY BILL HOO

The story of "Ascent" is about the metamorphosis of a few discarded kitchen doors, found table legs, some old specimen trays and even a few firewood scraps into a case of drawers on a stand.

Our voyage began on the street near my apartment where I found a pile of solid-oak kitchen cabinet doors, which I speculated had been originally installed in someone's kitchen in the '80s. As it happened, I had been contemplating a design for a case of shallow drawers wide enough to house tools or drawings – about the size of a collection chest or a flat-file holder.

I already had the perfect candidates for the drawers. For some time I was collecting discarded specimen trays that Harvard University Museum of Natural History was giving

away for free. These trays made from pine, fir, hemlock and cedar once held a variety of scientific specimens, from insects to rocks, and from ants to dry flowers. Impressive and sturdily built with finger-joint construction they endured decades, if not centuries, of use before being retired to make space for a more modern archival system for specimens.

Together with the doors and trays I also planned to incorporate four mundane table legs I'd saved from the trash. Unattractive and bulbous, I knew that after a complete overhaul these legs were destined to become part of the stand that would carry the case of drawers.

Working with objects of existing dimensions such as frame-and-panel doors can be challenging. My plan was to

Designing with Reclaimed Wood **139**

The old table legs, before re-turning.

Resizing the old doors by edge-gluing strips of reclaimed poplar to widen and lengthen as needed.

add material to the doors as needed, rather than dismantling them, milling the parts, and then reconstructing them. Instead, I milled reclaimed poplar strips to the same thickness as the doorframes, and glued them to the existing frames to increase their length, width or both. Then I connected the modified reclaimed doors together to make the case's box; one modified door became the lid.

To create a homogenized facade for all the specimen trays, turning them into proper drawers, I added false fronts made of maple. Interestingly, the maple strips were previously used as display signage in our local woodworking supply store. In one of my shopping visits I saw them sticking out of a Dumpster and decided to redeem them.

After the case was done I sketched out designs for the base, plus additional sketches to figure out how to sculpt the carrying wings and rods that would allow the case to be carried and lifted in and out of the base. Still more sketches dealt with ways to reduce leg thickness, which I eventually re-turned and reshaped into more elegant elements.

I carved the wings out of walnut reclaimed from a firewood bin, and hung them on the chest via bedrail hardware. The legs and the rails, meanwhile, are connected by robust bed bolts that allow them to be disconnected for long-term storage or to facilitate a more compact shipping situation.

The author dresses the finished case with a handplane.

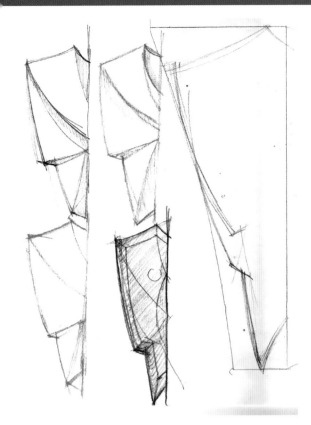

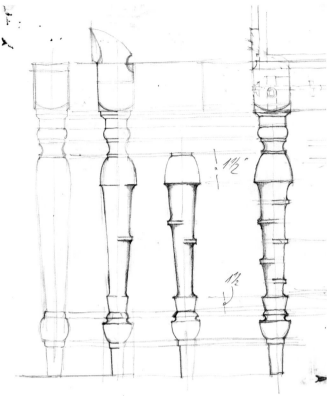

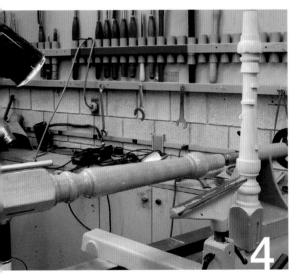

4

Re-turning the old legs. Note the completed reshaping on the right.

5

Cutting the aprons for the cabinet base on the band saw.

6

Shaping the aprons.

The completed base.

Carving the wings – a marked workpiece on the left, a completed wing, with mounting hardware, on the right.

Ascent is a great example of the power of reforming reclaimed furniture components and bringing them together into a new harmonious composition. It also demonstrates that painting this gestalt of mundane or "anemic" reclaimed elements proved to be a very effective approach. The paint allows us to appreciate the piece's unified proportions, shapes, and details rather than the mishmash of different woods species that were connected together out of necessity.

The completed "Ascent" cabinet, ready for final painting and the front door.

MULBERRY TRIO

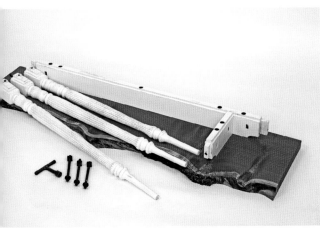

In Mulberry Trio, I installed a Salvaged/Recovered slab from
a storm-felled mulberry tree over a base made from found
legs. The legs I found in a Dumpster at 3RD Ward, a design
and educational workspace that used to operate in Brooklyn,
N.Y. To keep the project totally reclaimed, I also made various table components out of some odds and ends of reclaimed
wood scraps.

I have always been fascinated by contrasting or juxtaposed
elements in design, which, once brought together, generate
a visual outcome that none of the individual entities could
have produced on their own. As matter of fact, if paying close

1

The mulberry slabs came from Re-Co Bklyn, a New York City source for urban reclaimed wood, storm-felled trees and trees that had to be cut down because of disease. Learn more about ReCo-Bklyn in Chapter Five.

A Dumpster-diving find, these legs were perfect for the table.

attention to our surroundings, we're able to notice many facets of designs made of contrasting properties. These can be both man-made objects or natural: plants and animals. Think about a hermit crab and its shell, two separate entities – one alive, the other a salvaged empty seashell that provides a home and protection for the fragile crab. Or a juxtaposed white tapered swirl of ice cream over a crunchy brown cone.

Juxtaposition is present in architecture and furniture design too, and it's achieved via contrasting materials, colors, shapes or the combination of them. Take the Statue of Liberty, for instance, where the oxidized green gown descends over the rectilinear carved stone pedestal. Though the hierarchy is clear – the statue is above the pedestal. The pedestal, designed by Richard Morris Hunt is saturated with symbolism and architectural indications aimed to literally and figuratively elevate the Gustave Eiffel masterpiece to its rightful place in history. The base and the statue are made of different materials and forms, and yet they complement each other.

I believe that when designing an object made of two main components that are in close relationship, but are constituted

Trying to find the right legs and top composition.

Before painting, you can see the "sandwich" of reclaimed maple, mahogany and teak in the fabrication of the apron T-truss, which carries the top.

Bed bolts secure the legs through the "bolt pedestals" on the face of each leg top.

of different design vocabularies, it is often beneficial to introduce an additional degree of separation via color. I call this principle the "two degrees of separation rule."

In the case of Mulberry Trio, the top, made from a quartersawn New York City tree, provides organic warmth, while the white legs and rail, made from re-formed oak, teak, maple and mahogany, facilitate a sense of classical and austere order. To fabricate the apron "T" truss, which carries the top, I used reclaimed strips of maple, mahogany and teak that "sandwich" together to make a thicker beam.

If the base of the piece wasn't painted, its eclectic woody nature would have competed with the top and confused the viewers. By painting the base with an opaque color I was able to harmonize the entire piece and at the same time highlight both the natural live-edge slab, and the contrasting architectural base that carries it.

To add visual cohesion to the meeting point between the robust leg bolts and the legs, I built a wooden pedestal and glued it to the top face of the legs. The pedestal provides a respectable seat for the wide bolt head which connects the legs to the "T" truss.

Drilling the hole for the bed bolt through the leg pedestal and into the apron.

ATTN: JOHN EVERDELL

The original pile of reclaimed wood, just waiting for an idea.

"ATTN: JOHN EVERDELL" BY YOAV LIBERMAN
Cedar, pine, cherry, fir, sapelle, brass, steel, cotton-linen fabric, milk paint.
32" x 22" x 60"
PHOTOGRAPHS BY YOAV LIBERMAN

This story is about the evolution of a project from its infancy as a pile of scrap lumber and some very vague ideas about how it is supposed to look and be built, to its maturity as a cohesive creation standing firmly on all four legs.

It all began when a shipment of claro walnut for a dining table arrived at my friend John Everdell's studio in Medford, Mass. The cedar crating protecting this beautiful lumber from shipping damage was the polar opposite of what it carried: the boards were dusty, wrinkled, cracked and flaking; some were falling apart. After John broke open the container and extracted the walnut, the crating went into the Dumpster.

"When I saw those boards in that scrap bin I was immediately intrigued by the complex texture and coarse character of their mud-cracked, earthy appearance. I knew right then I had to make something with them."

Colleagues, friends and customers know I'm an avid

Dumpster diver and a strong advocate of using recycled materials and discarded wood in art and design. As such, most of my pieces are made from rejected wood or abandoned items. As a chef creates a meal based on the ingredients of the season, I meld the material I acquire to create a completely new and interesting piece that pays homage to the individual history of its ingredients.

So when I noticed the unusual coloring and remarkable texture of the discarded boards, I immediately sensed that their mission had not yet ended. Rather than being burnt or mulched, perhaps a better fate awaited them. Close examination revealed an interesting surface texture mimicking dry desert mud, earth colors and traces of dehydrated fungi, or perhaps a plant. And while the distorted surface gave hints about its long-term history, a shipping address written in permanent marker on one of the boards denoted its more recent

WHAT'S IN A NAME?

"Attn: John Everdell" is named after my mentor and friend, John S. Everdell, one of America's best cabinetmakers. John's splendid designs are deeply anchored in the Arts and Crafts vocabulary, informed from details found in Chinese furniture and refined with themes present in Greene and Greene aesthetics. John is a great innovator of joinery details. His repertoire of expressed joints includes many from Gustav Stickley's palette. But John has devised and crafted many more, including furniture legs combining wood and brass, tied together with unique connections.

He is also a great "wood painter." By this, I mean he is able to assemble a harmonious piece from a collage of parts – different species, dark and pale, flatsawn, quartersawn, spalted, curled – you name it. It was in his shop that I discovered the beauty of heart pine, the attractive characteristics of pear, and the wonders of claro walnut. And it was the remains of his packaging crate that triggered this piece.

These finger-jointed specimen trays became the drawers for this project.

use. I was even more pleased when I saw that, and decided that no matter what I built from this wood the addresses would remain visible.

"When I find an interesting object or an attractive piece of rejected lumber (attractive, to me, anyway), I first store it for some time not only to let it acclimate to the shop's climate, but also to let it 'ripen.' As with fine wine, this ripening allows me to experience the object differently and discover its new destiny. Of course, ripening takes time and storage space. Sometimes these treasures stay on the shelves in my cramped studio for years."

A few months later I spotted a pile of discarded drawers. Constructed of pine and with finger-jointed corners, these shallow drawers bore brass plaques declaring what they used to carry: specimens from the famous Harvard University collection of insects, rocks and fossils. These were from a similar batch of trays I later built my project "Ascent."

I'd always wanted to build my own version of a highboy.

For complexity and historical resonance, highboys are recognized by many as the ultimate achievement for a cabinet-maker. Highboys reign supreme among American furniture because of their size, elegance and impressive presence. Although the highboy originated in Queen Anne's England, it reached aesthetic heights in the New World. This visual legacy informed the conceptual framework of my highboy.

For some time, I'd considered building a highboy from some discarded metal drawers I'd found (in a Dumpster, of course). But when I saw the abandoned wooden trays and remembered those intriguing cedar boards stored in my shop, I knew they'd be part of my first highboy and started thinking about how to incorporate them into my grand scheme.

I now had drawers for my highboy and lumber for the case. But most of its overall design – the scale and proportions, the base section, the pediment, the hardware and color – was still undetermined.

Most of my raw materials are objects I'm inexplicably drawn to, either because they exude a sort of integrity or because I am saddened to see them abandoned. I'm especially inspired by the hidden potential in objects that have become redundant. I sketch, contemplate, and sketch some more, in order to design new elements that reincarnate the found items into something new, functional, and aesthetically interesting.

The amount of cedar lumber I had, factored in with the number and size of the drawers I intended to incorporate, governed the size of the upper cabinet, but at the time there weren't enough drawers to include some in the base. That meant my highboy's base would be a simple stand comprised of legs and aprons.

The theme

Throughout my woodworking career, I've been building furniture that can be stacked up, disassembled or recomposed due to my fondness for the compact, portable campaign furniture – a style of knock-down furniture, historically designed to accompany scientists, explorers and military personnel while on the move. In addition, I enjoy devising new fastening techniques that rely on dedicated hardware that augment my furniture. As a cabinet on a stand, my highboy was a perfect candidate to be forged in the campaign-style.

"The 19th century saw the golden age of campaign furniture. This is beautifully catalogued in 'British Campaign Furniture: Elegance Under Canvas, 1740-1914' by Nicholas A. Brawer, a splendid compilation of information, illustrations, and images of furniture pieces designed to travel the world. Although primarily built for Westerners, campaign furniture and its descendants now reside in dwellings and office spaces across the globe."

Campaign furniture was originally used in tents or temporary lodging, so it seemed natural for my highboy to have a tent overhead. While pondering the tent theme, I made an early sketch depicting a red canopy made from red Boy-scouts

Joinery for the case corners.

Attaching the drawer runners.

scarves that I'd found. But all that red was just too dominant and wouldn't compliment the base's color scheme I'd chosen – "soldier blue" milk paint – so I concluded that a plain linen canopy was best.

The case

I started by resawing the inner faces and edges of the weathered boards to create even surfaces for jointing. Once jointed flat, I glued the boards together to make the parts for the case, then cut half-blind tongue-and-rabbet joints. Before gluing the components together, I installed the drawer glides into dados cut into the case sides. Each drawer received a new false front made from the remnants of the cedar boards.

"The diverse coloration and sensational texture of the boards I'd rescued was so interesting that they deserved to be exposed, rather than removed or hidden. When lumber is transformed into boards and parts for furniture it's typically peeled, cut, smoothed and finished. I wanted to show that sometimes this process is actually unnecessary, because the beauty is already right there on the natural surface."

The base

In 2003, I built a bed frame (seen earlier in this chapter) with knock-down legs attached by means of two-way, bolt-rein-

forced miter joints of my own design. The rails fit tightly to create wedged corners that registered square to the legs, with two lag screws locking the joint, which proved to be very strong. I hadn't seen anything like it before, so I decided to explore it further in my highboy by creating a novel joint that literally showcases outstanding fasteners.

"Most builders prefer to hide joints and fasteners, even in this neo-Arts and Crafts era. Like earlier craftsmen, however, I prefer to expose and celebrate them."

After numerous sketches of joints I settled on a design using a decorative eyebolt that threaded into an insert sunken into the legs. Trapezoidal grooves machined into the rails match profiles cut in the legs. Tightening the eyebolt wedges the rails against the legs.

While working out the joint details, I also sketched leg profiles. I eventually settled on a two-sided tapered leg with a tall spade foot but I decided to present it inversely, just like the wood on the case.

The details

Like the finest highboys, mine has turned finials, but my finials aren't just decorative. They support the linen tent that serves as the pediment.

After discovering that I wasn't very good at sewing, I asked

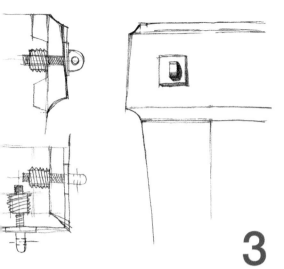

3

Designing the knock-down corner joints.

4

A closer look at one of the removable bolts in the completed corner assembly.

5

Cutting the leg profiles on the band saw.

6

Refining the legs with a handplane.

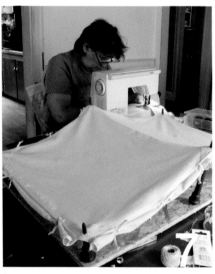

7

Sewing up the tent canopy for the top of the highboy.

my talented friend and fellow artisan Leslie Hartwell to fabricate the tent. To complete the piece, simple pulls adorn the drawer fronts, while salvaged tool-chest handles became the perfect "campaign endorsement" for the case sides.

"Studio-furniture makers wear several hats. Sometimes we merely execute functional designs that fulfill their duties honestly and diligently. Sometimes we're allowed the creative freedom to marry form and purpose. And sometimes, we set sail into the uncharted waters of art and creativity, striving to shape sculpture that functions as furniture (or at least appears to be functional), so it can be categorized as "sculptural furniture." When I saw that writing on the distressed cedar boards – the address of a man I respect so much, and in whose shop I've had the privilege to apprentice – I knew they presented a meaningful artistic and creative opportunity. I felt very strongly that I needed to reinvent those boards in a way that would honor this inspirational artist and the time I've spent working under his guidance."

CHAPTER 8

Epilogue: Reclaiming the Future
The gardener from Kfar Giladi

Reclaiming our future can only happen by evolving our society. And among the best agents of change are our children, to whom we will pass our baton in hope that they will do well.

In early 2018 a passionate woodworker and four school kids from a small rural community in the Upper Galilee region of Israel completed a yearlong reclaimed-wood project. Meeting once a week at the end of the school day, the small group of elementary school children from kibbutz Kfar Giladi worked hard to build their own storybook playhouse. Kfar Giladi is a collective agricultural community of a few hundred members near the Lebanese border in one of the most verdant and picturesque parts of the country. Surrounded by Mediterranean woodlands of oak, terebinth, pine and cypress that grow on the hillsides and mountains, and willows and sycamore trees which polka dot the valleys and the banks of streams that feed the Jordan River below, the members of this small community learn to cherish nature's gifts early on in life.

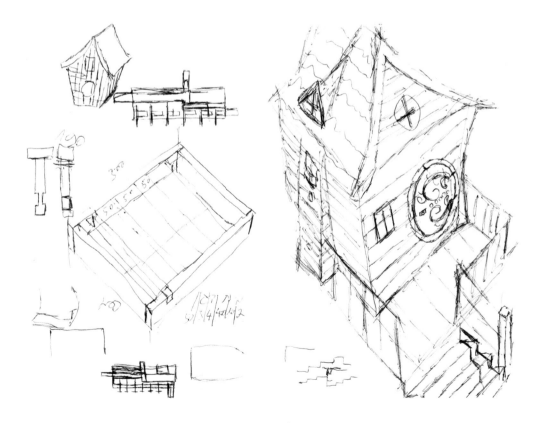

The design of the playhouse was very organic in nature, and evolved naturally as part of the process. These early sketches, for example, showed a round door similar to something a Hobbit would use.

Measuring and layout of the floor joists making up the playhouse's foundation.

Wooden equipment crates from the Kibbutz's mineral and limestone industry were dismantled for building materials.

Beginning with an idea

The storybook playhouse project began in 2016 and spanned just over a year. Ran Rabino, who heads the kibbutz's landscape operations by day, volunteered to guide a weekly extracurricular activity in woodworking throughout the year. His intention was to devise a project that would excite the group and provide a platform to teach them about team effort, self-reliance, building ethics and, of course, the craft of woodworking. He hoped that via this endeavor, the children would not only learn basic carpentry and woodworking, but also be immersed into the world of reclaimed wood and its vast potential.

Ran credits his mother for whetting his appetite for building and making things. From a young age he remembers watching her and learning how to work with wood and clay, erect masonry walls and more – much more. As was custom in the kibbutz, young Ran was asked at the age of 12 which field of work he wanted to apprentice. While others chose to take care of the livestock or learn how to plow the fields, Ran's natural choice was the woodshop – and he reports that it was a great decision.

Years have passed and although Ran no longer works in Kfar Giladi's woodshop, he retains an inseparable connection

to trees in his capacity as the community's head gardener. Being in charge of cultivating and stewarding the trees making this kibbutz's landscape so precious makes Ran's life meaningful. When one of his trees reaches the end of its life, he considers hauling it to a nearby sawmill and turning it into lumber. This Salvaged/Recovered lumber will later be used for building structures and utilitarian objects the community might need.

The kids and Ran set up a weekly meeting in the fall at the location of their future playhouse. Occasionally, when the weather was uncooperative (winters in Kfar Giladi can bring about some cold weather and even snow), they worked among the gardening gear in the landscape shed. Inspired by Ran, and supported by other kibbutz members, they started collecting all kinds of reclaimed wood, but especially Common Reclaims such as pallet wood and construction leftovers.

Slowly, but surely

The playhouse took shape slowly – much of the work was done with hand tools – but they created a wonderful structure exemplifying the best tenets of teamwork, artistic vision and passion for wood, craft, reclaimed ethics and aesthetics. As the work progressed, more reclaimed materials were spotted

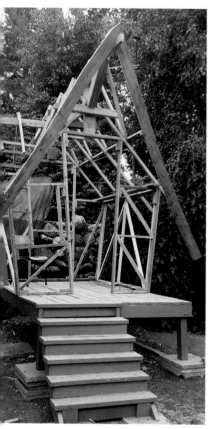

The upper structure begins with the basic framing, followed by the exterior walls, and finally the gabled window and railings.

and incorporated into the design. A storm-felled cypress tree was processed into shingles. Old wooden crates were dismantled and used to build walls and floors. And then, there was the industrial-sized chicken coop.

As members of an agricultural community the kibbutz elders and their descendants remember times of extreme scarcity, so it's not surprising that they're more conscientious than most with regard to resource use or abuse. On top of regular recycling and the separation of organic matter for composting, the community designated an old industrial chicken coop as a special "take it or leave it" location – a place for free exchange of retired items and equipment, similar to those described in Chapter Three. You see, kids, both young and young at heart love to find treasures, and so it is unsurprising that the "take it or leave it" venue played an instrumental role in the playhouse project.

When a cypress fell during a storm, Rabino salvaged the wood and used it for the playhouse's shingles and other exterior elements.

Roofing the structure.

As the project evolved and more people saw how enthusiastic the kids were, additional donations of reclaimed material poured in from members of the community. Moreover, a few kibbutz members offered their time and talents to the project to do chores that demanded a higher level of skill or just heavy lifting. By the end of the project, the inspiring work of Ran and his young disciples helped spread the "reclamation gospel" throughout the entire community.

A view toward tomorrow

It is through initiatives like this and the collective effort of individuals, companies and organizations, including those mentioned in this book, that we're able to embark on a reformative process to heal our world, or at least improve our immediate communities.

I believe that a prosperous future for our planet is only possible if makers, designers and consumers fully take into consideration the impact of their decisions and actions on the environment.

▲ This unique system of knobs operates the door's sliding bolt. When the six knobs on the left are turned correctly, interior shafts line up to allow the bolt to be slid to the side by the main knob, "unlocking" the door.

The completed door, ready for mounting. ▶

Reducing consumption, increasing product quality and longevity, taming down the irresponsible chase for new fashions and fads, reclaiming the discarded and rehabilitating the old and worthy, will pave our way for a sustainable future. Perhaps one the most effective ways to steer our society toward a more conscious consumption and intelligent resource use – and reuse – is by educating our younger generation to love and appreciate the wonderful gifts that nature has given us. It is through this conviction and the work demonstrated in this book that we can achieve this transformation of minds and hearts.

And nothing is more important than beginning with our children, as is so nicely demonstrated by the story of the kids from Kfar Giladi and their inspirational woodworking teacher.

INDEX

About the Author

Yoav S. Liberman has been a furniture designer and wood-worker for over 20 years. Trained as an architect, Yoav is deeply interested in all aspects of design and its impact on the world we live in. He is passionate about reusing discarded wood and found objects, and is known for his achievements in building modern knock-down Campaign furniture and innovative metal hardware. His pieces have been exhibited in galleries and museums in the United States and abroad.

As a writer, Yoav has published articles on woodworking and design in *Woodwork Magazine*, and *American Wood-worker*, and is currently a featured blogger for the Popular Woodworking.com website.

Yoav's pieces have been featured in Lark Crafts' "500" series of books, including "500 Tables," "500 Wooden Bowls," "500 Cabinets" and "500 Judaica," as well as in "Mind & Hand: Contemporary Studio Furniture" (Schiffer Publishing 2012), and in "Robin Wood's CORES Recycled," (Schiffer books 2015). Yoav is also a tool inventor whose design for a magnetic drawing and measuring tool was put into production by Lee Valley Tools, Inc., and his most recent wood-working tool – a handle that adapts machine-based mortising chisels to handheld use – is made by Rockler, Inc.

Yoav created and led the Woodworking and Creativity Program at Harvard University's Eliot House (2003-2011) where he taught seminars in woodworking and furniture design for beginning and advanced students. He was also an adjunct faculty member at Shenkar College of Engineering

and Design in Israel where he developed and taught core classes in furniture design and material studies.

Yoav served as a Windgate Foundation Artist in Residence/Fellow at Purchase College, N.Y. He was also an Artist in Residence and instructor at the Worcester Center for Craft in Worcester, Mass. He enjoys sharing his enthusiasm and experience through teaching at summer programs held at Peters Valley School of Craft, Penland School of Crafts, and Snow Farm – The New England Craft Program.

Yoav lives in Chestnut Ridge, N.Y., with his family and teaches woodworking at the Rudolf Steiner School in Manhattan.